Arthur Murray's

POPULARITY BOOK

Arthur Murray's POPULARITY *Book*

CONTENTS

You are not born with it. It's something you can acquire through conscious effort and personal honesty.

A Sure Way to Acquire
PERSONALITY

by A. H. Kulikowton
Condensed from OPPORTUNITY MAGAZINE

ALL KINDS of books on "how to develop your personality" are pouring from the presses today. Writers everywhere are turning out articles on personality development. Hundreds of teachers are giving personality courses. More than 500,000 Americans are enrolled in "personality schools." And yet—

No two authorities seem to agree on what personality is. One writer says that personality consists of those qualities which mark you off from other men, which make you stand out in a crowd. Another writer takes the opposite view. Personality, he says, consists in the characteristics which make you one of a group, an easy mixer, a good fellow among other good fellows.

One writer says that you must learn to dramatize yourself. Another insists that you must subordinate yourself, and display an interest only in the other fellow, if you want to make him like you. One man lays down rules for personality development. Another insists that there are no rules except: "Be yourself."

Now let's see, what are the facts?

The facts seem to be that all these points of view are right, and no one of them is completely right. "Personality" is a broad and inclusive term. Many apparently contradictory statements—all of them true—can be made about it. Personality is not a simple quality; it is a paradox. For example:

Here is a woman who most of us would agree has either an unpleasant personality or no personality at all. By that we mean that she does not impress us at all or that we dislike her. And why do we dislike her? Because, we say, she is shy. She is "introverted." She is "self-centered." She is "riddled by inhibitions." In short, she won't meet us half-way to establish a friendship. But now look at her side of the story—

Why is she shy, introverted, ill at ease? Why won't she meet our friendly gestures half-way? Because she knows—or believes—that people do not like her. She avoids as many human contacts as she can because she is afraid that she will fail to make the right impression. Yet it is her fear—and in many cases her fear alone —that prevents her being well liked.

The way out of that paradox is simple. Get over the fear of being disliked and you won't be disliked. The cure is to remove the cause. *Get over your shyness and people will like you.* And knowing that people will like you, you can easily get over your shyness.

Here's another paradox. We say one man has a good personality because he's the kind of person we'd like to have as a friend. We like the way he talks and acts, the stories he tells, the smile he wears, the way he does business. And, on the other hand, we say another man has a fine personality because of the way he treats us. If he is interested in us and our problems, if he lets us take the center of the stage, if he permits us to expand and to show ourselves at our best, we think far more of him. Thus on the one hand personality depends on the kind of a man he shows himself to be, and on the other hand on the way he treats us. Which is the secret of personality?

Neither—and both. A man with a good personality must be both interesting and interested in us—genuinely interesting and genuinely interested. It's that one word "genuinely" that makes all the difference. A man may wear the broadest smile and tell the most thrilling tales of his own experiences, and yet if we feel that he is being insincere or affected, we tend to dislike him.

Similarly, he may show the greatest interest in us, our families, our interests, our stories, and if we feel that his interest is forced, assumed or artificial, we instinctively shy away from him. Only the man who can treat himself and us as well in a genuine, straightforward, open way can be said to have a good personality. If he is being honest with himself and with us, we don't care whether it is himself he dramatizes or us.

And there seems to be a third paradox about personality. Each of us wants to be "personable," to be able to make friends and to influence others. But isn't it also true that we want to avoid being influenced by others, especially by their personality? If we choose a doctor, don't we want the most capable doctor, not the most likeable? And if we are buying goods, don't we want to buy from the man with the best merchandise, not from the man with the most glowing personality?

At first glance that seems true; but I don't think it really is. A doctor without personality, one who simply prescribes in a cold-blooded and disinterested way, isn't going to inspire faith and confidence in his patient. Without faith and confidence, the patient isn't going to follow instructions. It isn't likely that he will recover quickly. On the other hand, the doctor with a real personality, able to inspire confidence and able to interest people, will have his instructions obeyed more easily. More of his patients will recover. He's the better doctor.

The same is true of salesmen. The salesman with inferior merchandise can't be friendly and open-hearted. If he doesn't believe in his own product, he can't persuade others to believe in it. He may fool us when we are off our guard, but if we watch closely, we can tell a great deal about a man's product through his sincerity—in other words, his personality.

Moreover, the friendly man with the broad smile and charming personality is one from whom we are most likely to get service or adjustments if they are necessary. We feel confident of this.

Cultivating your personality means merely making yourself more likeable, making yourself into the kind of man or woman more people would like to have as a friend. Personality is not, therefore, something you are born with; it's something you can acquire through conscious effort and personal honesty. Get over your shyness; be yourself. You can do it, and you must do it if you want to be happy, make friends, and succeed. That is the reliable and sure way to personality — one which will be as natural to you as your own face!

* * * * * * ⟳⟲ * * * * * *

She's a Wise Woman—

Who keeps in mind that a little credit is a dangerous thing.

Who is able both to mend her husband's clothes and his ways.

Who has learned the paradox that to have joy one must give it.

Who can tell the difference between her first child and a genius.

Who most admires those eyes which belong to a man who understands her.

Who acknowledges the allowance made by her husband by making allowances for him.

Who appreciates that the largest room in any house is that left for self-improvement.

Who manages to keep not only her house and her temper, but her servants and her figure as well.

Who can distinguish between the laugh of amusement and the one meant to show off a dimple.—Adapted from Nancy Craig's *Woman of Tomorrow Program* over NBC.

4

More than mascara should meet the eye of anyone who looks at you. Your eyes are a mirror and to be alluring they should reflect your personality

What do your Eyes Reveal?

by Margaret McAnan   ❈   ❈   Condensed from the DES MOINES REGISTER

SOME psychologists judge character by studying the shape of the eyes.

According to theory, if you have round eyes you are probably innocent and trusting, affectionate, likeable and as unsophisticated as a kitten.

If your eyes are oval-shaped and wide, this theory says, you are not so easily fooled, but you are temperamental, emotional, poetic, a dreamer and an idealist.

Those whose mirrors reflect long, slanted eyes are declared to be secretive, clever without possessing great brilliance, sensitive to personal hurts, but unsympathetic and cold in their treatment of others.

If you have large, protruding eyes, you may be a rather bombastic person. You are probably suffering from extremes of generosity and selfishness, and are strongly opinionated, strong in your likes and dislikes.

Your emotions are supposed to be coated with frost if your eyes are small, oval and piercing. But don't let that bother you, because accord-

ing to some psychologists, you are quick-witted, keen-minded, even-tempered and so-oo suave! ·

Persons with extremely scientific minds, it is claimed, usually have deep-set or closely-spaced eyes.

Those who possess creative or artistic minds are supposed to have eyes that are rather far apart and wide.

Psychologists pay small attention to the color of the eye's iris as an index to character, but here are some legendary "facts" for you to remember or forget:

Gray eyes: depth of character and of feeling; reserve.

Blue eyes: honesty; humor.

Brown eyes: tenderness; warmth of feeling.

Hazel eyes: versatility; amiability.

Green eyes: daring; courage; gayety.

But even science admits that there's more in an eye than shape and color. None of us wants the windows of his or her soul to reveal an unfurnished house within. And it takes more than mascara and eye-shadow to give us optical oomph. Expression is nine-tenths of the eye and here are some eye-deas that may or may not lead to its possession:

When listening to a bore, it's a good idea (provided he's an important bore) to keep a lot of lively interest peeking out of the eyelids, even though you're wishing he'd choke.

Masculine eyes betray true feelings more than feminine eyes. This may mean that men are more honest than women—but it probably means that men are poorer actors.

Women can get away with a lot more eye trickery than men can. The closest a man can get to eye-suggestion-technique without looking silly is a bald wink.

A woman can glance coyly upwards through her lashes and look completely captivating to a gullible male. Lowered eyelids make a woman look either mysterious or demure (depending on her type). Lowered eyelids invariably make a man look sleepy (regardless of his type).

Don't mistrust the poor fellow who can't look you in the eye. It may only be the result of the failing mark he got in first grade. And the staunch and steady starer-outer who always gives you an eye for an eye isn't always the most trustworthy. The worst fabricator I know could out-stare an owl at midnight.

Boys who've made good will tell you that your own eyes can go farther than Dale Carnegie to help you in winning friends and influencing people.

But don't forget that it's the way they look *at* persons rather than the way they look *to* the public that really counts.

Overcoming Self-Consciousness

Many people are seriously handicapped by self-consciousness. They are generally at ease and well poised when with friends or close associates, but become paralyzed when obliged to meet strangers. They can't think of the right thing to say, are at a loss to know what to do with their hands and, in their own eyes, are awkward and ridiculous.

If you are self-conscious, and you make the effort to conquer it, you can succeed. Fear in the presence of strangers causes a feeling of inferiority. Such fear is usually without foundation. If the truth were known, the person you meet is probably as self-conscious as you. Realize that you are not in a position of inferiority, and stand up as an equal to strangers. If you can do this, your troubles will be over, for you will be able to act as freely and naturally as you do when you are with friends. And, by doing so, you will put those you meet at their ease.—*Weekly News Review*.

6

Whether you call it appeal, chic or glamour, charm is simply a state of mind based on self-confidence. Mastery of the three c's will bolster your assurance

Are you attractive to Men?

by Margaretta Byers   *   *   *   Condensed from DESIGNING WOMEN

IF YOU have charm you don't need anything else," said Sir James Barrie, "and if you haven't charm, nothing else matters much." Elinor Glyn called that indefinable something simply "It." The French call it chic. The fashion magazines call it distinction. The stage calls it appeal. Hollywood calls it glamour. Business calls it personality plus. Alice Hughes defines it as "something between cosmetics and clothes with a dash of confidence thrown in." Whatever you call it, it starts with a state of mind, and induces a state of mind in others ranging from feminine envy bordering on despair, to masculine admiration strong enough to make men jump through hoops—or more practically, jewelers' doors—as if they were bewitched.

Now this state of mind is largely self-confidence, which is a very different thing from vanity. Vanity is over-assurance—a calm assumption of the divine right of beauty—an atti-

tude that is irritating to men and women alike. On the other hand, an inferiority complex makes others as uncomfortable as it does the complexee. But self-confidence is something else again—a feeling of pride in the job you've done on yourself. It makes for gaiety which is attractive. It begets poise.

We can't go around simply willing men to swoon at our feet. To bring about this state of mind needs outward expressions through beauty culture, costume, and carriage.

To begin with beauty culture: If we can manage to look at ourselves objectively as mannequins do, we need not worry about other people's assets. We know we can do a lot with our own. When we have finished the requisite grooming of hair, and hands and skin, if we have some feature that is not conventionally beautiful, we can take the bull by the horns and stress that feature; make it an arresting accent, more exciting than cold,

7

conventional, accepted perfection. Ilka Chase once pointed out that the glamour girls are never pretty. They are interesting and that, of course, is the modern ideal of beauty. People are just beginning to realize the truth of this principle although it always has been true. The great sirens of history were 'not perfect. Cleopatra's nose was too short and it proved much more piquant than the classic noses of her Roman rivals. Katharine Hepburn, who certainly is not lacking in self-confidence, stressed her generous, drooping mouth with make-up that made it even more so. Garbo, whose straight, long hair presented a problem, finally let it hang in the long bob that was copied from coast to coast.

So remember, nobody need be unattractive or old today. The beauty salons can do anything. One of the smartest women in the international set boasts that she is the ugliest woman in Paris. She swears she looks like a monkey. But actually, she has made her irregular features provocative to the point of fascination. So, you see? The more discouraging your features, the greater the challenge to your ingenuity and taste, and the more potential distinction you have to work with.

Next, as to costume: We can express our love of beauty and cultivate that expensive look that is due our well kept complexions, hair, hands and figures. All this helps to make us feel desirable, and look it. Of course, it is up to the individual to decide

Nobody need be unattractive today. Provocative features, rather than perfect ones, are the modern ideal of beauty and the smart woman who discovers how to meet the challenge of irregular features can achieve compelling distinction.

just where to draw the line; just where rank extravagance begins for her. But bear in mind that out-and-out frivolity is not wasteful if it bolsters up your ego. Psychologists realize that these things are necessary to feminine mental health. They're much more effective than tonics and so much easier to take.

Perfumes give you value received when they give you a lift. Furs are worth more than the actual warmth they provide if they make you feel distinguished. A bit of good jewelry is worth its price, if it helps your morale.

Even luxuries that don't show at all are worth their price of admission into this country from nations that have a better understanding of women. A woman's frivolous indulgences —her bath salts that bubble like champagne, her body lotion for a stimulating rubdown, her toilet waters, sachets and extravagant lingerie —all give her a feeling of being rather precious herself, which is her birthright and the best possible insurance against nerve disorders. We have

8

come a long way from our Puritan beginnings. Today, a woman is commended for spending money (within reason) on herself. It is expected of her in business and in social life. It is an investment that brings cash returns as well as intangible satisfactions.

And, finally, as to carriage: A woman's bearing expresses her state of mind more eloquently than any other one thing. They tell a story about Ziegfeld, watching his girls as they passed in review. He was considering them for a certain bit. Eventually he chose the least beautiful of the lot. Asked why, he said: "She feels beautiful." And she did. She carried herself proudly. Her gestures were relaxed and therefore flowed gracefully, one into another. Her state of mind created an illusion of beauty.

Often you can work from the outside in. A new hat will make you hold up your head. High heels will make you walk daintily. A well-cut costume gives you something to live up to and you will stand better instinctively. But all this ought to be part of your feminine equipment. You should not depend on clothes for your beauty. Dancing schools teach girls to manage their feet, and gymnasiums help their postures. We'd like to see every school include a course in stage deportment to teach girls what to do with their hands so they won't be at a loss later, unless fortified with a cigarette and a cocktail glass.

You may think all this terribly affected. Of course, it will make you self-conscious until you've mastered it. But you should practice deportment secretly in front of a mirror until it becomes second nature. Our physical culture expert says:

1. Stand up with knees relaxed and rotate them slightly outward. (This will bring your hips together.)
2. Hitch your tummy up and in.
3. Drop your shoulders, flatten your back and up comes your chest.
4. Throw back your head and tuck in your chin.

If your shoulders are back and dropped, your arms cannot hang straight and limp with simian awkwardness — they suddenly become part of you and you discover things to do with them.

We suggest, if your hands are still bothering you, that you watch a model as she shows a dress. She doesn't hug her bag; she changes it about from hand to hand. She adjusts her fur scarf, and so on. You will notice that it helps to carry something. Probably that's why British army officers carry swagger sticks, and elegant ladies walk their dogs. In the evening a chiffon handkerchief, or even a flower plucked from your corsage, gives you something to cling to. So much for the rudiments. When you've mastered them, you're ready for the subtleties.

The art of wearing clothes depends on an innate feeling for them. Actresses and the best mannequins never wear a costume without rehearsing in it before a mirror; studying the best way to tilt a hat, suiting their walk and gestures to a coat or suit or dress,

9

practicing how to manage a train, draping a wrap or fur scarf, getting the feel of the clothes, so that unconsciously they will play up to them.

Hope Williams wrote an article about this some years ago. She told how she altered her whole bearing for different costumes. In a suit, she would stride across the stage to stand feet apart, arms akimbo, with her back to the fireplace. She would unbutton the jacket and put her hands on her hips, almost like a man clasping his hands under his frock coat tails. In a military dress, suit or coat, she would march as smartly and stand as erect as any West Point cadet. In chiffons, Miss Williams became quite a different person. She seemed to float rather than walk, her arms found softer, more picturesque poses.

These tricks remind us of the smartest mannequin in New York City. A certain merchant said she was worth a fortune to him. She wasn't conventionally beautiful. But she loved clothes. She would hug a wrap to her as if to say, "Don't you adore it?" And she sold the clothes right off her back.

If women would only cultivate this feeling for clothes it would give them a much wider scope. When a woman says, "I can't wear clinging things," it may be because she doesn't know how to be a clinging vine herself. The more of this flexibility she can develop, the more of the various roles she can assume. Every woman is a bit of an actress at heart. So why not cultivate that talent? It's refreshing, both to her and to her audience.

So much for the three c's of "That Indefinable Something" for which charm is as good a word as any—cosmetics, costume and carriage (including clothes - consciousness). We promise you they will make all the difference between resigned self-consciousness and serene self-confidence.

What Men Think of Women

In a survey conducted by Henry F. Pringle in *The Ladies Home Journal* a majority of the men of America said that:

Married men are happier than bachelors—78%.

Good companionship is the most attractive quality in a woman—68%.

Women, after marriage, do not make enough effort to keep themselves as neat or as charming as before. Women, however, *do* remain as sympathetic.

Men prefer brunettes to blondes—59%.

American women are spoiled—55%.

Men and women should equally boss the home—53%.

Women should hold jobs before marriage—91%; but not after marriage—90%.

Today's women give too much time to things outside the home—59%.

They know how to manage the family money—54%.

HOW TO MAKE A MAN *Propose*

by LILLIAN G. GENN

IF ANY MAID doesn't make her dream of love come true—there's always a reason! And it needn't be because of her looks, her clothes or her bank account. These things help, of course, but we all know that there are many girls who haven't these assets who nevertheless manage to make a matrimonial conquest.

We discussed this great game of courting and marrying with David Seabury, who is one of the foremost consulting psychologists in America. He is the author of such best sellers as *Growing Into Life, How to Worry Successfully, The Art of Selfishness,* and many other books.

In his new one, *Build Your Own Future,* he shows what new techniques in living can do to get us what we want from life. And so we asked him, what about a girl who is missing

romance? What is the source of her trouble, and what techniques can she use?

Mr. Seabury is a tall, distinguished looking man with a warm, friendly manner and twinkling blue eyes. He relaxed in an easy-chair in his New York office and spoke quietly, but with zest.

"There are scores of young women who long to marry," he began. "They dream, hope and strive to win love, yet in many cases these girls hold attitudes toward men that frighten love away, some point-of-view of which they may be unaware but which, expressed, would make any prospective husband wary.

"There are three such important mental attitudes or ways of looking at life. First is the girl's interest in marriage itself. That is, the desire to be married rather than an interest in her own development and a determination to become so desirable that it's certain she will marry.

"The second is some unconscious antagonism toward the masculine sex.

"The third is where there is some one of the typical mental and emotional maladjustments such as an in-

11

feriority complex or persecution feeling that interferes with successful human relations. It's obvious that the self-conscious and hypersensitive girl isn't an easy and natural companion, and that the feeling of frustration and depression which comes from her lack of popularity interferes with any man's making a successful contact with her."

In order to understand why a girl may remain unmarried, Mr. Seabury elaborated on these three attitudes.

"I've put an interest in marriage first on the list," he said, "because it's by far the most serious handicap. Let me make a parallel. You've seen the type of man who wants to have money, but doesn't really want to work for it. He wishes some distant relative to die and leave him a fortune, or he hopes by some lucky fluke to gain riches. But he isn't the least interested in making himself so efficient an employee, so dynamic a personality that he eventually rises in the world and becomes successful.

"Similarly, many a girl is interested in marriage rather than in developing into such a vital personality that not one, but many men will want to marry her. She thinks that marriage is something which good fortune may bring or something that she herself can secure by maneuvering and planning. Her real interest is in the institution. She wants to be a wife, mistress of a home, mother of children and to have a good provider. And although she doesn't know it, when she's interested in this way in the marital relationship, she's not actually interested in love. Consequently she doesn't make herself available to love.

"Today it's much harder to interest young men in marriage. When a man meets an attractive young girl, his hope is to avoid rather than to achieve that happy consummation.

"He knows that he must assume plenty of responsibility," said the psychologist, "when he marries. And while he may be willing to do this for love, few men want to carry such burdens merely for the possession of a home and wife. He also wants to be sure that his marriage will be successful. Moreover, he feels that too many girls just want to get married, and after a few years, they don't care anything about the husband. They

• *The woman who makes the winning and keeping of love, and not marriage, her aim, is the one who wins marriage. The old tricks of coquetry are outworn; the desirable woman of today is vivid, alert. She intrigues a man because she is temperamentally wide-awake and takes part in things with him, feels with him, grows with him.*

look upon him as an adjunct to pay the bills.

"On the other hand, a girl feels that she can't be sure of happiness either. Today she can support herself and get some happiness out of life. She doesn't need to be a slave to any man.

"I've already spoken of the second cause of failure to marry. The average young woman has a good reason not only to fear marriage but for scepticism as to the worth of any relationship with a man. She's quite aware of the fact that she's still living in a man's world. She may be supreme in her home and more protected by law than the man is if anything goes wrong with marriage. But she's still placed in a dependent position by both nature and society.

"Therefore, how the man treats her, his tenderness and consideration are more important to her than general virtues are to him. He can get out of the home easily enough and find solace in the world. But the unhappy wife is in no such fortunate position. Her unconscious fear thus prevents a girl from giving her best to win a proposal."

The girl who solves her problem under present conditions is the one who makes herself desirable.

"The old saying that bees go for honey is still true," smiled Mr. Seabury. "And if she uses her imagination so vividly that what she says flashes with interesting pictures, or if she is so wide-awake in the use of her senses that she brings into her conversation a sense of the thrill of life, she becomes the kind of companion that intrigues a man.

"I don't mean to imply that a man wants a highly intelligent woman, but he doesn't want a sleepy one. It's not the woman's logical capacity or her profundity of thought that's important, but her mental vivacity.

"It's the woman whose feelings merge with her imagination and her sense of alertness, who interests the modern young man. He wants a woman who can take part in things with him and feel with him. He still enjoys being something of a monologist. He wants to tell his troubles and ambitions and to paint pictures of the future. And he's still thrilled by the 'Aren't you wonderful' technique," twinkled Mr. Seabury.

"A man is likely to turn away from the girl who is concerned with herself and how she feels. He doesn't want the girl who always gets her feelings hurt She must learn to take it and never mind how she is being treated.

"It's a new test and an important one. She must not only be a vivid and vitally interesting creature, but she must be a human being first and be tested out by life. The girl who can't take it, won't get married. The vital development of her own nature and of her mind rather than the old coquetry, is important.

"The woman who makes the winning of love and the keeping of love her aim, and not marriage, is the one who wins every time. She does it in her desire to grow rather than to acquire tricks. The average man today knows too much about women and sees right through any tricks."

Here Mr. Seabury outlined a practical technique to help a girl make her dream come true.

"She should first study the women who have been successful. She should see what makes them desirable. If she merely imitates their behavior, she'll be a poor second. She needs to understand more deeply some of the important laws of human behavior and learn two of them that are essential.

"One is what we call the image-making process; the other the actuation process. If you wish to change your behavior, make mental pictures when you go to sleep of the way in which you wish to behave in the different types of situation which are likely to develop in your life.

"For example, a young girl is too self-conscious and nervous in her relations to men. She has seen women who are confident and at ease with men. When she goes to sleep at night, she can picture even the details of her conduct. 'I am going to speak this way and act this way,' she says. She visualizes the natural, easy grace and feminine charm which she wishes to acquire.

"By this visualization process she is creating a series of what we call activity patterns which will ultimately impress themselves on her will. If along with this impression of mental pictures she also acts out her new behavior insofar as it is possible, if she makes herself do the things that she believes will better herself in relation to people, she actually stimulates her thought and feeling to flow along the new channels."

That this is no mere theory has been proved again and again. There is a firm psychological background for belief in such a means of fulfillment.

It's just like building a house. First the architect makes the plans and the builder then goes to work and puts them into action. Our changes of conduct will begin to pass in the same way. First make the design for your behavior. Use suggestion to possess it and put it into operation. This is the key not only to successful living, says David Seabury, but to those changes that may be necessary for the woman who wants to bring love into her life.

WHEN you want someone to think highly of you—let them know how highly you regard them. If you say: "Gee, you did that well!" . . . the other fellow is going to think that you're a pretty smart person. Sincere praise acts like a magnet—and pulls admiration right back to you.

ARE YOU A GOOD GUEST?

Condensed from THE PSYCHOLOGIST

PERSONAL RELATIONSHIPS and social contacts are acknowledged to be important to successful living. It is well worth considering how we treat our friends' hospitality.

As you answer the questions below you will immediately see whether you make a selfish visitor in other people's houses, or if you are the truly welcome guest. Answer "Yes" or "No" to each question.

1. Do you make a point of arriving punctually when invited to a meal?

2. Can you decide what is the best time to leave, and go without lingering?

3. Do you realize your responsibility for contributing intelligently to the conversation?

4. Are you always careful to avoid arguing or airing your views to your host?

5. Can you, without being too personal, show a real appreciation of the provision for your entertainment?

6. Do you, to save your host embarrassment, leave food fads at home?

7. Do you talk of other people's interests more than of your own?

8. Have you ·really absorbed the fact that being entertained is not merely accepting a treat, but consists also of fellowship and *mutual* enjoyment?

9. Do you avoid, even privately, looking around to criticize your host's belongings and taste?

10. Do you try to make the gathering a success, rather than concentrating on "making a hit" yourself?

11. Do you refrain from doleful observations on the weather, the international situation, etc.?

12. Have you tried to learn, and observe unobtrusively, such points of etiquette as make for good manners?

13. Are you equally courteous to those present, irrespective of age, sex, or class?

14. If any little hitch occurs do you try tactfully to help smooth it out, rather than leave all responsibility to your host?

15. Are you soon invited again to a house after your first visit?

Add up your "Yes" answers and find if they are more than the "No's." To what extent the negative or affirmative answers predominate should be of definite interest to you.

I know that dancing is more than just recreation or an attractive exercise. It is a magic that transforms the shy person into a self-confident and poised person.

My Inferiority Complex

I had ten jobs and was fired from every one. Not because I did not try hard, but because I did not have what it takes to make good . . .

by ARTHUR MURRAY

I WAS excessively tall for my age. At fifteen I was five feet eleven, and painfully self-conscious. We lived in New York, and my home was on the East Side, where youngsters are not noted for politeness. "Hi, skinny!"— "Hello, stringbean!" were remarks dinned regularly into my sensitive ears, making me all the more diffident and unhappy.

Perhaps it was my self-consciousness that made me very shy. At any rate I was shy—and shyness brought about a certain backwardness and gawkiness, so that at such parties as I was invited to, and at school gatherings, the girls all ducked me.

I was quite miserable, and eventually my work at school became affected. And the fact that through illness I didn't graduate from public school until I was almost sixteen, added to my humiliation and unhappiness. Youth was an unhappy time.

After some months at High School I could stand it no longer. I thought I was too old to be in the first year of High School, and of course my height was still a source of keen embarrassment to me. By this time, too, my awkwardness and diffidence had become pernicious habits. I decided to quit school—and my parents reluctantly agreed.

Within the next six months I had ten jobs and was fired from every one of them. Not because I did not try hard enough, but because I did not have what it takes to make good: Assurance, Aggressiveness, Poise.

My parents then advised me to go back to school. I did so, and was more discouraged than ever. The girls shunned me, and when I couldn't resist looking in at a dance, I was a wallflower.

Finally a girl in my class took pity on me and offered to show me some steps. Because I was awkward and ill at ease, I found it hard to learn. But she had patience, and in due time I could dance.

This achievement—for it was an achievement!—gave me a keen sense of liberation. I was more like other boys. And I loved dancing. It seemed to bring me out of myself. But, the thought of going to a school dance still frightened me.

Out of desperation came a plan. The immigrant colonies on the East Side celebrated their weddings with dances. I selected a wedding where I was sure I would not be known, and barged in. After watching a while I picked up the courage to ask one of the girls to dance. To my surprise, she smiled and agreed.

That dance was a delight and a revelation. Here I was dancing with a girl, leading her easily through a crowd, mixing with scores of other dancers—and no one thought me out of place! No one thought of my height; no one said I was clumsy. I was just like anyone else in the hall! It was a wonderful sensation.

I went home that night, happy for the first time in many years. And from that time on I haunted the East Side weddings. I still lacked the courage to dance with acquaintances. But outside of my own neighborhood, I was becoming bolder and bolder. Then something

extraordinary happened. One of the settlement houses gave a ball at which a prize was offered for the best dancers. Inspired with a superhuman daring, I entered the contest.

My partner and I won the prize!

In that moment of victory my confidence in myself was firmly established. When I left the settlement house I was a free youth, knowing that I could associate with others on an equal basis. So sure of myself, in fact, did I become, that I brazenly applied for a job as an instructor at a dance hall—and got it! That was how I made a start in my profession.

And because I suffered so much myself through supposed deficiencies, and because it was dancing that released me from what threatened to be a life of bondage, I can well testify to the therapeutic value of dancing.

My own case reminds me of that of a girl who came to us, very much depressed. She was unusually tall—six feet. In an attempt to make her height less conspicuous she had fallen into the habit of stooping slightly, and this gave her a sort of hunch-backed appearance.

ARTHUR MURRAY *once qualified for the title, "World's Most Awkward Young Man." In this story he tells how dancing released him from the bondage of awkwardness and self-consciousness.*

Through the liberating influence of dancing, Arthur Murray—a tall, gawky, bashful boy at 18—emerged from his cocoon of obscurity to be America's foremost dance instructor. Dancing can work miracles!

But the teacher was quick to detect any virtues that the girl, Edith, might have as a dancer, and to praise them. And by the time her first lesson was finished, Edith had become extremely interested. There was a new light in her eyes, color in her cheeks, and her body had straightened out perceptibly. The music and the dance steps had given her a feeling of exhilaration that was already apparent in her manner and posture.

Edith came to us for a half hour every day, and each day she became a more normal person. In time she became a really beautiful dancer. Her height was an asset rather than a detriment, and it was a pleasure to see that tall, slender figure move through the graceful patterns of a tango or glide with smooth swiftness to the strains of a Viennese waltz.

She no longer came into the studio with her head down and her lips set sullenly. She held herself erect and proudly. When she entered a room it was with the awareness that she would make a favorable impression. That gave her new confidence, and a certain graciousness that added immeasurably to her charm.

All of this was the result of the liberating influence of dancing. Dancing had forced her to exhibit herself, and in so exhibiting herself, she had forgotten her inhibitions. Dancing had brought her companionship—and through companionship she had discovered that people saw virtues in her that she had not suspected she had.

Dancing, in short, had transformed

"It's time for your Rumba lesson"

her from a shy, inarticulate girl into a poised, self-possessed young woman.

During the 30 years in which I have taught dancing, I have known any number of people whose lives have been radically improved by dancing. And I have become convinced that this art should not be looked upon merely as a recreation or as an attractive exercise. There are qualities in the dance which far surpass mere entertainment or exercise. The dance is a vitally important factor in our social plan, the American way of life, and should be acknowledged as such.

I only wish that the public generally were as well aware of this value. I believe there would be many more happy people if it were.

At social gatherings do you stutter, tremble, blush? Develop an "other-consciousness" and in no time you'll overcome self-consciousness

ARE YOU Self-Conscious?

by Milton Powell ✳ ✳ ✳ Condensed from THE PSYCHOLOGIST

SELF-CONSCIOUSNESS can be observed in people of all ages. But it is more likely to attack the young boy or girl than the more staid or "settled" middle-aged man or woman.

In young or old, that awful feeling of social embarrassment is a quite unenviable experience. Many people through self-consciousness, blushing, and the like have completely spoiled their chances in life. Advancement and promotion are hindered and social life becomes a torment.

No real enjoyment of the company of the opposite sex is possible, contacts with useful superiors are avoided, even life in the shelter of the family can be tainted by this weakness. Time which ought to be devoted to productive thinking is given instead to a miserable, unprofitable introspection, to a timid and shrinking concern over the next occasion for appearance in public.

The physical symptoms may be blushing, sweating, trembling, shifty or averted gaze, halting speech, hesitant manner, or a hurried "I-want-a-quick-get-away" manoeuvering.

Many and varied are the occasions on which self-consciousness is painfully evident. Ridicule, severe reprimand or criticism, or even praise will cause the crimson tide to flow into the cheek. Facing a crowd, meeting prominent people, being subjected to a question of integrity or honesty, meeting a disliked person, being introduced to members of the opposite sex, are all experiences which may give rise to self-consciousness.

On every one of these occasions the self-conscious sufferer has to attempt an approach to and a relationship with other people. This puts us at once on the track of the causes of the trouble. Certainly the primary cause of self-consciousness is a failure to establish a right social contact with others. Those people who never suffer from self-consciousness developed the right attitude to acquaintances, friends, crowds, toward strangers. They are always at home, "at-one" with people.

What prevents the self-conscious sufferer from meeting his fellows with a perfect mind and social ease? The primary reason is failure in social adaptation. The secondary causes of this failure are as follows:

1. *Egocentricity:* In every instance the self-conscious person can be shown to be far too engrossed with himself and his own feelings and too little concerned with the interests and feelings of others. He suffers from too much "in-thinking." He lives too much within himself.

He may tell us that he goes about doing good, helping others in a kindly way, yet his self-consciousness does not abate one jot. His interest in others is as yet not really deep and powerful enough to outweigh his interest in himself.

2. *Lack of Objectivity* is a common enough cause of self-consciousness. This means that the self-conscious sufferer fails to see a situation as it actually is. Let us suppose he starts work on a new job. He feels that he is the cynosure of every eye, that all the older employees are watching him, and that his employer especially has him under close observation.

Yet this is probably far from being the real truth. They have their own many duties upon which to concentrate, and, in fact, bestow upon him only the most fleeting and casual attention. Obviously, the right objective approach to a new job would

be expressed in some such formula as:

"Here's my new job. I must learn it with courage and patience, not seeking to make an impression but to put all of me and the best of me into doing it well."

3. *Fear of Social Failure:* Many who are physically brave in situations of real danger are rank cowards in a social situation. Call upon a winner of a bravery badge to give an after-dinner speech and he will very likely display all the symptoms of anxiety and self-consciousness.

If his social courage is as great as his physical courage, he will not let one little breakdown dishearten him or create a habit of self-consciousness. Rather will he seek occasions on which he can practice public speaking and learn to feel as confident in that sphere as he did on the field of battle.

4. *The Fear of Not Creating A Good Impression:* This keeps thousands of people from attempting tasks in which they might readily excel. It also spoils the attempted work, for really good work cannot be done while the attention is distracted by the unspoken thought "I wonder if I'm doing this to the satisfaction of the onlookers. How awful if I fail!" This self-watching attitude is fatal. When we become conscious of a beating heart it beats still more rapidly. Even our physical organs "dislike" being watched.

During adolescent years the bugbear self-consciousness plays most havoc with social poise and peace of mind. In the first place, the emotional life at that period is less stable, more sensitive, less under control. The mental and moral powers are not yet fully developed and in control of the emotional self. The adolescent boy is not yet fully adapted to social environment. He is no longer a wholly dependent child, but on the other hand, he may not have won complete independence from his parents or in the occupational sphere.

Often his parents are too critical, too exacting, too domineering, and this discourages and disturbs him. He does not yet feel equal to the many and varied demands and adaptations which society imposes upon him.

The adolescent is often very egotistic. He thinks he knows everything. The result of this is that he is unwilling to be taught and is especially sensitive to any criticism. He takes every correction from his elders or superiors as a personal insult or affront to his intelligence, and shows this by every sign and symptom of self-conscious annoyance.

A particularly annoying and extremely common form of adolescent self-consciousness is that associated with the opposite sex. This is due largely to a lack of practice in social living. Perhaps the only cure is for the adolescent to go as often as possible into the very society most feared. Often sheer repetition, making what was formerly a rare occasion into a matter of common routine will work wonders. This is where such social mixing as is promoted by mixed games, swimming parties, club socials, and dancing performs a useful task in social education.

The chief aids to the self-conscious, then, will be:

Take far more interest in the lives of others. Be less concerned with how you feel and more devoted to your task, your plan, your problem, your friends. Practice social-mindedness so much that eventually it drives completely out of you all infantile or adolescent self-centredness.

Self-consciousness smothers one's native powers; "other-consciousness" expands and develops and strengthens them. You *can* overcome your self-consciousness.

Do YOU KNOW how to give graceful compliments—the kind that make people like you? Here's the secret . . . put the "you" in each remark. Don't say: "What a smart looking outfit you're wearing" . . . say instead: "How smart you look in that outfit."

FOR MEN ONLY

MAKE A HABIT of using a few drops of good toilet water or lotion when you dress. Don't forget . . . a girl's nose knows, too!

How to Carry on an

INTERESTING CONVERSATION

by *Ethel Cotton*

HAVE YOU ever stopped to think that your happiness and your success in life depend to a great extent upon your ability to carry on an interesting conversation? Do you realize that the people who get their salaries raised, or are promoted to positions of power, or are popular at social gatherings, are those who talk engagingly and distinctively?

Conversation is the game of social contact in which we toss ideas to and fro for the two-fold reward of pleasure and profit. Only those taking part can fully enjoy the exercise. Each idea has the power of entering any number of minds simultaneously. At the same time its essence still remains with the sender. Conversation is thus a game in which no one who plays can lose.

The first principle in the technique of conversation is: Don't be silent! If you are a chronic listener, people are apt to think one of two things: either that you are dull and have nothing to say, or, granting you have ideas, you are unfriendly or uninterested

and do not care to express them. On the other hand, if you do exchange ideas, you derive a keen enjoyment and an increased knowledge of human nature.

Second Principle: Don't chatter." Remember that "con" means "with." To converse is to talk "with" not "to" your friends. If you talk constantly and do not permit others to express themselves, not only will you be shunned, but you will fail to gain anything from social contacts. Listening is an essential part of social courtesy.

To avoid monopolizing the conversation, find a subject of interest to the other person. You must realize that your interests may not be of great moment to the person with whom you are carrying on a conversation.

Third Principle: Stay with the subject. If the conversation is to be interesting and valuable, the ideas exchanged must be worth-while. Dull or "rag-bag" conversation usually results from the introduction of unnecessary details or irrelevant ideas, or from a lack of intelligent selection and order. Conversation should never move in circles nor jump from subject to subject but lead to an end or at least move forward.

A worth-while topic should grow like an increasing snowball, as different people add their ideas. It is for you to guide or so control the subject that every one is eager and able to express his opinion.

Fourth Principle: Guide the conversation. Even though the subject may be of interest to the person who introduced it, unless the ideas have value for the others in the group, it is a courtesy to change the conversation.

A great deal of tact is needed in changing the topic which has been introduced. The conversation must be guided so diplomatically that the one who introduced the original subject will not realize that it is being changed.

Here are three practical ways to change the subject. Use the method or combination of methods which best fits the situation. As you acquire confidence and skill, you may create other devices of your own.

1. "That reminds me" method: Associate a new idea with the one which must be changed. For example:

Eight of us were at the beach. The day was foggy. Somebody began, "It really has been very cold this summer; we seldom have such a long stretch of cold weather without a few warm days between."

Someone else politely agreed and then said, "By the way, speaking of weather, did you know that a Columbia professor has evolved the theory that eventually the intelligence of people may be definitely measured by the temperature of the country in which they live?"

"It sounds far-fetched. How does he explain it?"

It did not matter whether or not we agreed. It did matter that a useless conversation had been diverted into an interesting discussion that led us into heredity, environment, racial traits, economic pressure, and other subjects far removed from the weather.

2. "Will you help me?" method: To halt a bore in mid-sentence, as it were, ask his advice about something. This must be done carefully and with proper apologies for interrupting him. The wish for advice must be sincere. This sincerity will be recognized by the interrupted speaker. Who would not willingly stop in the middle of his favorite subject if he felt his advice were needed at once on an important matter? This is an excellent method for diverting the enthusiast who is talking "shop" or a mother extolling the merits of her children.

"Children are so cute when they are four or five years old," said the fond mother, Mrs. Billings. "This morning, Johnnie...."

"Oh, before I forget, Mrs. Billings, will you tell me the date of the next Parent-Teacher meeting? I wasn't able to attend last week."

"It's on the twelfth," said Mrs.

Billings, absently, ruminating on Johnnie's genius.

Before she had time to revert to her subject, however, her friend continued, "And the speaker at the next meeting?"

"Professor Bacon, who is going to talk on Child Psychology."

"I am glad," said her friend. "I wonder if you will read this book and prepare a list of questions which we may present at the open forum after the lecture. Suppose we look it over now and decide which seem to be the most important chapters."

This they proceeded to do. An interesting conversation on the necessity of understanding child psychology followed.

3. "Isn't it beautiful?" method: While walking or driving with a group, you can change the subject by attracting the speaker's attention to some object sufficiently interesting to justify the interruption. Then tactfully guide the talk along more constructive lines, linking it, perhaps, with the object recently pointed out.

"This machine rides very comfortably. What make is it, Mr. Adams? Oh yes, a Buick. We had a Buick last year, but we decided to trade it in and get a Studebaker. I like a Buick myself but my husband likes . . ."

"Oh excuse me, but there is the Palace of the Legion of Honor. Isn't it beautiful? Suppose we go in for a few minutes."

After the visit to the Palace, other members of the group may take up the conversation with the history of the building, its architectural beauty, and various exhibits held there recently.

To acquire the ideas essential for conversation, you should carry a notebook constantly. Each day you should jot down at least one idea in abbreviated form. Divide your notebook into three parts under these headings: 1. Miscellaneous, including current events and things of transient interest, which are the subjects most frequently used in casual meetings. 2. Book Reviews and Authors, including thoughts and personalities prominent in the literary world. People are sure to mention things they've read. 3. Subjects of special interest to you or your friends, including the topics most likely to appeal to your friends.

This plan of gathering conversational material has two distinct values. It stimulates mental alertness and a sense of selective values as to what is worth-while. And, by referring to the ideas in abbreviated note form, you are compelled to think out the subjects imaginatively, strengthening your memory and power to recall specific details.

Test each of your conversational efforts by these questions: Is it chatter? Does it matter? If you plan the subjects for your conversations and direct the flow of talk according to the principles given here, you will be able to avoid those haphazard "rag-bag" chats that bore everybody concerned. You will be playing the game of social contact, gaining pleasure, profit, and popularity.

Here's a plan to make your personality give off sparks

6 WAYS TO WIN PERSONAL MAGNETISM

by Donald A. Laird

Condensed from THE TECHNIQUE OF BUILDING PERSONAL LEADERSHIP

A GROUP of ambitious management executives attended a conference in the Engineering Societies Building in New York City. Almost all of them were college graduates. They were well dressed, well fed, polished. Each stated his opinions carefully and fluently. The meeting reeked of logic. But it was getting nowhere.

When it seemed that the conference might break up with nothing accomplished, a shrimp of a man sprang to his feet. He wore poorly fitting, old-fashioned clothes. The other men seemed amused at his appearance, and when he began to speak in an accent like a Swedish comedian, they were even more amused.

Before he had uttered fifty words the dignified men were listening attentively. Their amusement had disappeared. Soon the little man had the group in the palm of his hand.

Why? Because he was the first to give off sparks!

The stuffed shirts had irradiated dignity but no sparks. The small man lacked looks, bearing and good speech, which the others had, but he had a priceless something the others lacked —a magnetic personality.

The little man was Carl Barth, the famous industrial engineer.

For a personal magnetism that wins people, be active, cheerful, exciting, brisk, direct and fearless.

Be Active: Fiorello La Guardia, mayor of New York City, has a magnetic personality. It has helped keep him in important offices for years. His short legs would be a handicap to many men who do not have his magnetism, but they keep La Guardia active, continually on the go. He wears out his shoes, not his trousers.

Don't get the idea that magnetic people were born with something different that makes them active. This activity is very often deliberately assumed. Billy Sunday, for instance, was a quiet fellow, who impressed the members of his family as a bit on the indolent side. But when he was on the platform, when he wanted to lead people, he made himself become active. He was, in a sense, acting. His jumping, gesturing, shouting were part of a deliberate plan to be active. He was not born that way—he made himself become active in order to lead others.

Magnetic women, too, have this asset. They are not languid leaners, striking statuesque poses. They are on the move, alert, almost restless. The trained actress cultivates this characteristic, and she can steal a scene from a more beautiful woman who lacks vigor.

Magnetic people show their activity in their handshakes. They use no "dead-fish" handshake, no polite finger touching. They use their hands to gesture when they talk. They put steam in their talk, and speak more rapidly than neutral people. Observe the popular radio programs for an object lesson in this; try to repeat the words right after the speaker and you will find he is talking much faster than is habitual with you. Magnetic persons keep their voices up at the end of sentences. This keeps listeners in an expectant attitude. Let your voice trail off and you lose attention. Magnetic people also give emphasis to some of their words. They pause a split second and then push out a word with more emphasis than usual. This is one of the secrets of Winston Churchill's power over his listeners; his talks sound like a military polka.

Be Brisk: One of the first habits Theodore Roosevelt formed deliberately, in his boyhood, was to be brisk without being brusque. He had a vigorous handshake but a brief one. His talk was brisk, too. He would talk actively for a few sentences, then stop in silence and let the other person carry on. His glance was brisk. A few seconds of intense concentration into the other's eyes, then to their hands, jewelry, chin. He was brisk at social gatherings, the first to excuse himself from friendly groups.

He left people expectant.

Neglect to be brief, and one becomes a bore. When Lord Dufferin arrived late at a luncheon, he apologized to the hostess by explaining that he had been detained by the Earl of Kimberley. Then he whispered: "A wonderful man! It is amazing how much he knows. He knows everything—everything!—all the corners of the earth and all the men in them. He knows everything, except when to stop!"

Be Cheerful: The radio programs with the high ratings are the ones that feature comedy.

People who have grouches or who let the corners of their mouths turn down are about as magnetic as an old maid at a bachelor party.

Will Rogers endeared himself to the entire world by his cheering face and words. His humor was a cheerful outlook on things others worried about.

I was in a small Georgia city one springlike Saturday. Two legless beggars were seeking alms on the public square. One was whining. The other had a mongrel dog, which he fondled as he smiled at the passers-by. I watched from a distance for a half hour. Eight persons gave alms to the smiling man with the dog. Two others gave to both beggars.

People who have personal magnetism must be cheerful. They talk about glad events, not calamity. They encourage others, never emphasize discouragement. No matter what obstacles are ahead, they talk and act success, not failure. Others feel better after a few minutes with such people. Just as the magnetic person leaves others feeling expectant by his briskness, so does he leave them in elevated moods by his cheerfulness, even when he has to pretend that cheerfulness. And more successful persons than you realize *pretend* they are cheerful.

Be Direct: A few years ago a blind student majored in my courses. Of the two dozen students, he was by all odds the most popular. He was, in fact, the most magnetic man on the campus. It was not because the students were sorry for Pat, either. He earned the popularity by being active, brisk and cheerful. So were many other students, but Pat's blindness, strangely enough, helped him to be more direct than any of the others.

Since he could not see those to whom he was talking, he spoke intently in the direction of their voices. He turned his face in that direction. He faced others when he talked to them and did not talk out of the corner of his mouth. Sightless, he spoke more directly to others than most people do.

The man who looks at the ceiling, out of the window, or at the third vest button is not being direct.

When a girl has beauty and background, *plus* directness, look out, men! One woman, for instance, wondered what Peggy Upton Archer Hopkins Joyce Morner had that she didn't have. Peggy Joyce, she is usually called; the other names she has won on the field of matrimony. The woman in question saw Peggy Joyce at a nightclub and watched her jealously. She thinks she discovered one of Miss Joyce's secrets of power over others.

When Miss Joyce and her escort were seated, she turned and looked carefully at the other tables. She satisfied her curiosity about the people who were there, whom they were with, and what they were wearing. Then she turned to her escort and never took her eyes off him for the rest of the evening.

You cannot be magnetic by talking to the ceiling or to the floor.

Be Exciting: It has been said of many outstanding men that they are leaders of men and followers of women.

A clean interest in the opposite sex is a mark of normal emotional development. Perhaps a fourth of adults lack this, and while they may be brilliant and accomplished they usually lack magnetism and leadership. Others, though having a normal interest in the opposite sex, spend their lives trying to suppress this perfectly natural interest; they become stiff, cramped, and nonmagnetic people.

The case of a scientist comes to mind. For years he had been conducting himself as if he had not yet been told the facts of life. As a prudent married man, he was so cautious that the womenfolk thought he must hate women. The men believed he had ice water in his veins.

He was shocked to learn that one of the most important ingredients in personal magnetism is a strong, yet idealistic and controlled interest in the opposite sex. He had been pretending to ignore women, when he should have shown his interest in them by many little gallantries.

Be Fearless: Anyone who has personal magnetism has a mind of his own. Such folk stand by their convictions even when they are not popular beliefs. The natural leader has the ability to fight, if necessary, for what he thinks is right. He speaks out against injustice, graft, obsolete methods, blunders by the high and mighty. This quality shows itself not just by sticking one's chin out when there is trouble around. It is reflected in the tone of voice, firmness of glance and lips. It gains respect for the leader—and wins followers to loyally carry through any project.

Once I was helping my uncle on his small farm. Thistles had sprung up in the hayfield, and he put me to work clearing them out. I approached the first one tenderly, then let out a yelp of pain as its nettles stung my hand. Although it was a blistering hot day, I set up a cry for leather gloves to handle the thistle.

"It's easy, if you know how," my uncle said. "Grab hold firmly, as if you meant business. That crushes the prickers. *Never pat a thistle.*"

✣✣✣✣ *Reading Your Profile* ✣✣✣✣

YOUR PROFILE, says Mrs. Nancy Van Court, is bound to fall into one of four classes. Here's how she reads them:

1. *The overcast type.* (Straight, dominant brow; receding chin.) This type has the judicial brow, the streamlined chin; cautious in thought, quick in action. He is energetic and impatient, sometimes hasty, but capable of great triumphs.

2. *The convex type.* (Sloping brow; receding chin.) This type is streamlined; quick in thought and action. If this is your type, you should be a complete success or a complete failure—no halfway business.

3. *The undercast type.* (Sloping brow; protruding chin.) This type is impulsive in thought, cautious in action. He has flash judgments, but doesn't trust them. He does things thoroughly, once he gets started.

4. *The concave type.* (Straight dominant brow; protruding chin.) This type is judicial; slow and careful in thought and action; reliable and methodical in details.—*The American Magazine.*

29

The Americanized Version of the Original Argentine Tango is a Simple Ballroom Dance... Easy to Learn

I HAVE arranged the Tango here so that anyone who has mastered the Waltz and Fox Trot (its steps are similar to those of these two dances) will be able to go on easily to it. The *original* Tango, which came from the Argentine, *was* a difficult step as was the French adaptation of it. The Americanized version is a simple ballroom dance which no one should have trouble learning.

The *deliberate* manner in which the Tango is danced will enable you to develop very quickly the necessary co-ordination between mind and feet.

The rhythm of Tango music is similar to that of the Fox Trot, but is usually played more slowly. The steps are divided into *slow* and *quick* movements. The *slow* step is given *two beats* of the music. The *quick* step is given only *one beat* of the music. This slow-quick variation is what gives the Tango a great deal of its individuality and charm.

TANGO

Your Way to Popularity

THE PROMENADE • WALKING STEP

MAN'S PART

1. Walk forward slowly on left foot.
2. Walk forward slowly on right foot.
3. Step forward quickly with left foot.
4. Step quickly with the right foot, diagonally to right.
5. Quickly draw left foot up to right, *no weight* on left. Pause one beat.

... *TANGO*

THE CHASSÉ • SIDE STEP
MAN'S PART

The steps are taken sidewise. The man has his back to the center of the room as he progresses to his left.

1. A long slow step with left foot to left side.
2. Cross right foot in front of left, weight on right.
3. Step with left foot to left side.
4. Draw right foot up to left, weight on right.

The first step is slow; the last three steps are done quickly. Repeat the entire step three more times. All steps are taken sidewise, to the man's left.

THE CORTE • OR DIP
MAN'S PART

1. Place the left foot forward quickly.
2. Quickly draw the right foot up to the left.
3. Quickly step back on the left foot, bending left knee, right knee straight. Raise right foot an inch from floor.
4. Slowly step forward weight on right foot.

The action of the left foot in the Corte gives the effect of a pendulum swinging forward and backward. Repeat the entire movement, beginning with left foot. The Girl should read the Man's part very carefully. When lifting the left foot off the floor, point the toes out and *backward*.

33

Samba

FROM the throbbing tropics of Brazil comes the Samba. Originally a tribal dance among African slaves, it was adopted by cosmopolitan Rio de Janeiro and adapted to the suaver, more sophisticated mood of ballroom dancing.

The light-hearted danceable Samba is one of New York's most popular dances, rating high in any popularity poll. We picture it here in all its poetry of motion as performed by the ace dancing team of Fred Astaire and Rita Hayworth.

BASIC STEP

Starting with left foot, take one step forward, weight forward, bending knee twice . . .

count   1   and   2   and
       (down) *(up)* *(down)* *(up)*

(The man's part is described throughout)

REPEAT STEP WITH RIGHT FOOT . .

count   3   and   4   and
       (down) *(up)* *(down)* *(up)*

It's a bouncey kind of step . . . the bending knee levers the body, the left shoulder swings forward with the left foot, the right shoulder leads the right foot.

Cutting=in

Cutting-in is the privilege of a man in the stagline and it has its own rules. If a man wants to cut-in, he asks the girl's partner, "May I?" The man dancing with the girl steps aside good-naturedly and the girl smiles at both men. It is rude to be overjoyed when some particular person cuts-in, because this suggests that a girl feels relieved at being rescued from her original partner. It is equally rude not to break.

HOW TO BEHAVE AT A DANCE

Your Degree of Popularity is Often Measured by
Your Knowledge of the Simple Rules of Etiquette

Dancing is a partnership pastime, usually enjoyed in a social group. For the comfort, convenience, and happiness of all the dancers, certain rules of the game have come to be recognized by well-mannered people! Some of these rules apply only at very formal dances while others are observed always. Generally speaking, the full enjoyment of dancing depends on simply living up to the Golden Rule—consideration of others, consideration of your hostess, and consideration of your partner.

Once you have accepted an invitation to a dance there are certain things you have automatically agreed may be expected of you. You are expected to be suitably dressed, pleasant company and—*above all*—able to dance.

This is not the place for a review of good manners, though an evening spent dancing is certain to display a person's knowledge of them. Therefore, I here tell you only points of etiquette that apply directly to dancing. In these points I purposely have placed the Formal Dance first and Informal Dancing later, as the etiquette of the Formal Dance covers *all* the traditional rules of the game for dancers. If you are familiar with them the etiquette for the Informal Dance becomes simply a matter of knowing which rules are observed less strictly on less formal occasions.

THE MARATHON CHAMP

At a formal dance, the Girl precedes the Man when entering the ballroom. A young girl follows slightly behind a chaperon, pays her respects to the hostess, then moves away to make room for other guests.

The Man does not take the Girl's arm when walking into the ballroom.

The Man always asks for the favor

of a dance. He says, "May I have the pleasure of this dance?" — never, "Have you the next dance?"

THE SHOW-OFF

It is bad form for the Girl to decline to dance unless ill or not dancing and she must not dance with one Man after refusing another.

The Man never leaves the Girl standing in the middle of the floor; he escorts her back to the patronesses, her chaperon, or friends, remembering that he must not lead her off by taking her arm.

After dancing with a Girl, if a Man wishes to seek another partner, he should leave his first partner with friends or a chaperon and first seek another gentleman to dance the next dance with her. He can leave his partner by explaining that he wishes to hunt a friend who is anxious to meet her.

Departing guests always seek out the hostess and express pleasure for a delightful evening. However, if leaving early and the hostess is engaged you may properly go without disturbing her.

When you converse, be tactful. Think of your partner's point of view.

Invitations written in the third person (Mrs. John Smith requests . . .) are properly answered in the third person. Informal notes can be answered by notes. A telephone invitation is either answered on the spot or a telephone call back (if the invitation was given to a third party as a message) is correct.

Invitations are sent out from two to three weeks in advance of the event. They should be answered within twenty-four hours after they are received.

It is grossly insulting to the hostess to appear at a function in anything but the proper dress for the occasion.

Décolleté is proper for a formal dinner dance, the elaborateness of the costume varying in proportion to the formality of the evening. Simpler clothes are worn to a simple party or informal dance. A young woman or debutante may be as elaborately gowned as a matron, but good taste suggests she use jewels more sparingly.

Beau Brummel's famous advice still holds good: "To be well dressed, you must not be noticed."

Formal evening functions demand white tie and tails. A white waist-

I'M JUST A NATURAL DANCER I GUESS

THE MAN WHO NEVER TOOK A LESSON IN HIS LIFE

THE WRESTLER

JAMES THURBER

coat is worn; patent leather pumps or ties go with this attire, both winter and summer. A top hat, dark overcoat and gray gloves are worn with full evening dress. White gloves should be worn at the opera or an evening dance.

For small informal dinner dances, dinner jackets may be worn with black bow tie; either black or white vest. For a formal dance in summer a dinner jacket may be worn with white flannel trousers, or white linen tuxedo jacket or short white mess jacket with black trousers.

In making introductions be gracious, avoid abruptness. A younger woman is always introduced to an older one, and an unmarried woman to a matron. "Mrs. Jones, may I present Mrs. Smith?" is correct.

Men are always presented to women, and the woman's name is spoken first—"Mrs. Smith, may I present Mr. Black?"

The simple acknowledgement is best—"How do you do, Miss Smith?"

A woman acknowledges an introduction to a man by bowing and repeating his name, though a hostess may elaborate this cordiality by offering her hand and repeating a name and expressing her pleasure in the introduction. A younger woman should rise to acknowledge an introduction to an older woman. If a woman is introduced to a group of women, they need not rise unless she is an older woman.

YOUR CHARACTER—

How Dancing Reveals It

There is nothing mysterious in reading character by dancing. Anybody with a sharp eye and a little imagination can have a lot of fun sitting on the side and figuring out his friends. When I watch dancers, I appraise them not only for their performance but for their characters. I am influenced by the expression of a person's dancing as some people are influenced by facial expression. Music and

Who turns his toes out is usually sensual, vain, self-indulgent.

rhythm put the conscious mind to sleep and dancers are in a state akin to hypnosis. The subconscious mind is nearer the surface than usual and some hidden things express themselves.

The key to good dancing, good character, and happy living is abandon, letting go, turning your feelings loose.

Men who try new steps and fancy steps, and race with the music usually make the best companions. And girls who fall into their partners' moods and travel with them make the best wives.

Beware of the partner who tries to outdo you in dancing. Dancing is mutual and the person who tries to do a dozen steps with a partner who knows only a few steps is an egoist and a fool. It takes a good character to dance well and what is most desirable in a partner is adjustability.

Men who point their toes while dancing are usually in love with themselves. If a girl is more interested in toe-pointing than the dance, she, too, is vain.

Men who stare into space and dance a beat ahead of the music are usually of artistic temperament; the dance itself has no reality for them. They may produce great works of art but make poor companions.

Dancers who set heel down first, then toes, plodding dancers, are egocentric and sure of themselves; often do well in business. They get one idea —or learn one dance step—and never change it.

Dancers who turn their toes out

Beware—a very primitive gesture—a symbol of possessiveness.

are usually sensual, self-indulgent, vain.

The most charming persons I have known were pigeon-toed. Check over *your* list.

The man most easily led holds the woman's hand in his up-turned palm.

Dominant men grip a woman's hand with an overclasp.

Thoughtful and considerate men usually hold a partners' hand in the way most agreeable to her and touch her back lightly with their fingers.

The aggressive, go-getting man with qualities of leadership, holds his partner firmly and lifts his elbows high —he may be an excellent provider but a poor companion.

The walking dancer who pushes his partner ahead of him around the floor is obviously dull and inconsiderate.

The man or woman always in search of new dancing partners indicates either a spoiled, fickle nature or an inferiority complex.

The man who dances with a sure, solid step and looks neither to left nor right — who waltzes his partner through the thick of the floor, bumping into others and making no apology —is both stubborn and stupid.

Persons who change their style of dancing frequently are not affected— they are the people who make prog-

Artistic men stare into space and usually dance one beat ahead of the music.

You've found a good-hearted, real person, who, though an old codger, has some good kicks left—some gaiety in the flick of the feet.

ress—open-minded, adaptable, courageous, and eternally youthful. The dancer who never changes his pattern is a trial to his partner and a bore.

The partner (non-professional, of course) who undertakes to correct your dancing is the vain and cunning type. He is trying to convince you that he is an important, kindly man and the female of the species is very maternal. She treats her partner as if he were a little boy just learning to dance, and if he falls for it he will dance to her music the rest of his life.

Elbows tell a lot: elbows down, no confidence; elbows up, sure of self; elbows high, proud and vain.

The loose-limbed, sloppy dancer may be a genius or an ass, but whatever he is he is irresponsible, carefree and indifferent to everybody, and himself.

The woman who cannot dance without a strong lead is timid.

The less sensitive dancer likes fast, march-step music—a beat for each step. The more intelligent, nervous type likes music that permits steps within the beats.

The person who prefers the abandoned dances, the rumba, tango and slow fox trot, is usually easy to live with.

Strait-laced people prefer the more formal dances—waltzes, fast fox trots. Important persons often make nervous, timid dancers.

There is more to the art of character-reading than watching for outturned toes and elbows held high—the feeling about the dancer which is difficult to define. It has to do with the dancer's movements; with the honesty and frankness of the stride and step; with the bearing and quality of the person. The thing in a dancer that catches the spirit of the dance, which is fine, free, generous, kindly and wholesome, reveals or reflects those qualities.

⁘⁘⁘⁘⁘⁘⁘⁘⁘⁘⁘ ◎ ⁘⁘⁘⁘⁘⁘⁘⁘⁘⁘⁘

HOW TO OVERCOME NERVOUSNESS

TRY TO DEVELOP a detached point of view. Nervousness easily becomes a habit, and those who are nervous by habit are invariably self-centered. If you keep personal feelings out of a problem, it becomes easier to solve.

Will power and self-control are good cures for a case of nerves. Substitute constructive thoughts for destructive ones.

Learn to control your emotions. Fear, anger, and worry not only harm your physical health, but make clear and sane thinking difficult.

Cultivate a spirit of optimism. Things might always be a great deal worse.

Help along your sense of humor. Try to see something amusing in all your difficulties, and when you start worrying needlessly, laugh yourself out of it.

Get the habit of being able to reconcile yourself to the unexpected little things, so that you can view greater disappointments with some equanimity.

—NANCY CRAIG on WOMAN OF TOMORROW PROGRAM, *National Broadcasting Co.*

the RUMbA

A MUST in the Dance Repertoire of Popular People

The Rumba, known in Cuba as "The Son," is unique among ball-room dances. It has a charm, an aura of seductiveness and mystery, all its own. Correctly danced, it is as smooth as the Fox Trot, as decorous as the Waltz.

The Cuban Walk

The slightly rolling hip movement, which Cubans have in their dancing, is the result of the manner in which they place their weight. In American dancing we do not have any hip rolling action. In the Fox Trot, for instance, when you take a step with the left foot, you immediately transfer your weight to the left foot. Hence, no hip motion.

But in the Rumba, when you step forward with the left foot, the weight should remain on the *right* foot, causing the right hip to protrude.

As you step forward with your right foot, the weight remains on your *left* foot. Note that the left hip protrudes.

Go back to the beginning and read carefully.

Now try walking around the room in this Cuban manner. (Place your hands on your hips and feel the hips swing from side to side.)

1. **Place left foot forward, weight on right.**
2. **Place right foot forward, weight on left.**

Walk slowly in this manner for half an hour without music. Then walk for an hour in time to slow Rumba music.

After you have mastered the slow Cuban walk to the count of: 1—left, 2—right, you are ready to do the Cuban walk more quickly.

Step quickly: left, right, left, pause. Count: 1, 2, 3, pause.

After practicing the forward Rumba walk for one hour, practice going backward in time to Rumba music: 1, 2, 3, pause. Repeat for one hour.

Cuba's National Dance ⟶

The Box Step in the RUMBA

● This is the oldest and still .the most frequently used step in the Rumba. The girl's part is the same as the man's. Note that you pause after 3 and 6. Practice for an hour.

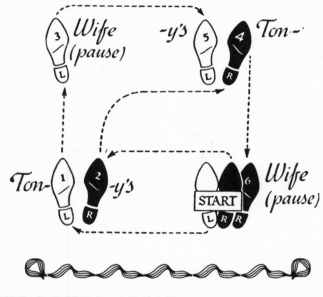

THE RUMBA BREAK

The Rumba Break usually follows the Box Step. (1) The man steps quickly back on his left foot, (2) transfers his weight to right, (3) then steps forward on left, (4) pauses, weight on left.

Note that as the man steps back on his left foot, the girl steps back on her right, and they break away from each other. She steps forward with right foot on 3, rejoining partner in closed position. Practice for an hour.

THE RUMBA TURN

In this Rumba turn, the man goes backward. The girl goes forward.

This turn usually is preceded by the box step. Do the turn for 12 counts, and end with the box step (6 counts).

HERE IS a simple way to dance in the typical Cuban manner: As you take a step—whether forward or to the side—let your *knees* lead.

But, when stepping *backward*, let the *toes* lead. (Visit your nearest Arthur Murray studio for a free demonstration of the Rumba.)

NOW YOU CAN *P*SYCHOANALYZE *Y*OURSELF *!*

by David Harold Fink, M. D.

Condensed from the book, RELEASE FROM NERVOUS TENSION

PSYCHOANALYSIS is a method of enabling you to understand yourself. It is a form of treatment that helps you discover your habit patterns, or your neurotic trends, in order to bring them under control.

Charming Lady Bountiful psychoanalyzed herself when her nerves were beginning to get her down. She complained about insomnia, palpitation of the heart, and wondered whether glandular treatments wouldn't help.

We agreed to try self-analysis. She began by writing on paper all that she did during a typical day. Her day proved to be a hectic round of errands, mostly senseless, that she was running for other people. For example, "Drove Mrs. Smith to the hairdresser," and "Took the two Jones children to the swimming club." I picked out these two items.

"Couldn't Mrs. Smith have taken a streetcar or a taxicab?"

"Yes, I suppose that she could. Only, I called her up, and when she said that she had to have a hair-do, I promised to drive her to the beauty shop."

"What did your husband think of your free taxi service?"

"He just jumped all over me. The tire situation has him upset, poor dear. He yelled at me so that I couldn't get to sleep."

"So, actually, you were generous to Mrs. Smith at your husband's expense."

"Well, I spent my time."

.I decided to talk about that later. "What about the Jones children?"

"But I had promised the children. Should I break a promise to them?"

"Here, again," I pointed out, "you were generous with your husband's car and tires and gas. And here again, you deprived those children of their opportunity to solve their own problems. Now go on doing as you have been doing, but keep track on paper of your daily round of activities."

In a week she came in with her report.

It included many trivial errands that she had run for people in whom she had no interest. And this is the point—from all her favors she was deriving not the least bit of satisfaction or sense of accomplishment.

"How would you characterize these activities in another?" I asked.

"Busybody. Minding other people's business. Trying to buy friendship and appreciation. Kidding myself into thinking that I'm useful." She began to cry. "And I'm so unhappy. Nothing that I do makes me happy."

"Then ask yourself why you do these things."

Within a week she had the answer. She had written, "I run around doing things for other people to keep from thinking what a failure I have been."

"Why do you consider yourself a failure? Don't tell me. Think about it and write the answer."

She wrote, "Doctor, I always wanted to be a writer. I never dared, because I was afraid of failure. I'd rather be dead than start anything and fail and have people laugh at me. I suppose that you will call this another of your neurotic trends, and say 'Why?' I know why. My father and mother were perfectionists. Nothing that I did was ever good enough to suit

Are you afraid to tell on yourself? Don't be. Self-analysis is one method by which you can discover just what it is that keeps you from achieving the fullest mental and physical health. It will enable you to readjust your thinking habits, banish your frustrations and find a real joy in living.

them. And I got into the habit of avoiding anything, even though I wanted to do it, for fear I might fail."

You will see in this progression of self-analysis how one neurotic trend after another was uncovered. First, the neurotic need to "help" others, which was revealed as resulting in activities that prevented others from leading their own lives and solving their own little problems. Then came the exploitation of her husband and others, using them to furnish the means of her apparent generosity. It's easy to be generous with someone else's money.

She adjusted to discovery of her neurotic trends by getting a job as a reporter on a newspaper. Her husband was delighted. "At last you're doing something worth while," he said. Perhaps she will never be any great shucks as a writer, but she is happy.

You can uncover your neurotic trends by going through the same procedure. First, make a schedule of the things that you do every day. You will discover that some activities are almost compulsive in character. Something within you makes you follow them. Put a check mark against these Pied Piper activities; they will bear investigation. Some of them may be useful, and they give you a feeling of healthy accomplishment. They are not neurotic trends. But there are other activities which make you feel like kicking yourself for having done them. They result in nothing but misunderstandings, quarrels, disappointments. They make you unhappy.

These activities are motivated by neurotic trends. Double-check them.

What drives you into these activities? Why do you do them? For example, do you constantly quarrel with your children? Is this a habit that you would like to break? Then ask yourself what neurotic trend makes you quarrelsome.

In one case, a patient quarreled constantly with his wife. An analysis of his behavior at the factory where he worked showed that he habitually dodged responsibility. Having to support a wife prevented his quitting his job. He lessened his job worry by quarreling with the wife. Fear of responsibility was the neurotic trend that kept him from having a happy home life with the woman he loved. That same fear kept him from getting ahead on the job that he could have enjoyed.

Your list of neurotic trends might include some of these:

"I have a compulsion to show off."

"I use illness as a means of getting my own way."

"I have an abnormal need for sympathy, which makes me tell everyone my troubles."

This list could be extended indefinitely. It is intended only to give you an idea of what is meant by a neurotic trend: a name for a group of unconscious habits that prevent you from being yourself.

No one likes to tell on himself. That is the difficulty you will run up against in your attempt to name your own neurotic trends.

There is a way to fight this tendency to see oneself through rose-colored glasses. You can become objective about yourself.

Take the case of the loving wife. She wouldn't let her husband see his old friends because they kept him up too late. She would call up his office to tell the boss that her husband could not come to work because he had a slight cold. She wouldn't let him read more than half an hour because she didn't want him to ruin his eyesight. Add up these and forty more items, and you come to one conclusion: the loving wife was trying to ruin her husband's life. And why that conclusion? Because in spite of all of her loving protestations, her behavior led only in that direction.

As if. Remember those four letters, those two words, the next time you go motive hunting. If your behavior is *as if* you wanted to fail in marriage, or in business, or in school, *as if* you wanted to hurt someone, *as if* you had to put on a false front, you don't have to look any further for your neurotic trend. Evaluate your motives in terms of *as if*, and you'll come up with the right answer.

Once a woman observed, "It looks as if I *wanted* to be a chronic invalid, doesn't it?" She wanted me to say "No." I said, "You do, or you wouldn't act like one." The truth helped her. Treating her as a chronic invalid would have prolonged her disability.

After you have made the exciting discovery of your neurotic trends your next step toward freedom is to ask, "How did I acquire these emotional habits?" The answer is to be found in your childhood conditioning. Go over the story of your life. Write an autobiography in twenty or thirty pages, not a pretentious one, but something a little more in detail than what you would write in an application for a job. Don't be afraid to tell on yourself. Get at the facts of your early conditioning that established the habit patterns that you regard as neurotic.

Mere awareness of neurotic trends is not enough. You must do something about it.

Freud thought that sexual repression was at the root of all neurotic behavior. In Hitler's Germany, however, where sex is free and easy, but where freedom of speech is hammered down by secret police, neurotics will have fear complexes about the expression of one's opinion.

Modern medicine, however, avoids all philosophical "schools" of thought.

Self-analysis is one method by which you can discover what it is that you do that prevents you from enjoying your own highest level of physical and mental health. It should enable you to readjust your activities, your frustrations, and so establish habits of thinking that will give you greater joy in living.

Are you in Love with Love?

BEFORE you take a dive into a white satin gown with a rose point lace veil—before you culminate that spring romance with a garden wedding—ask yourself these questions. They were prepared by Dr. Henry Bowman of Stephens College. By the time you have checked your real emotions against them you should know whether or not *he* is the man or whether what you have been feeling is just a little "seasonal magic."

1. Do you enjoy each other's company better than anyone else's?
2. Do you like to do the same things together?
3. How do you make up after a quarrel? What kind of conflict do you have and what is the significance of this conflict?
4. Are you willing to make concessions to him? Do you forgive his shortcomings? Do you tolerate them?
5. Does he wear well? How does he fare in competition?
6. How easily and how readily do you publicize what ought to be private?
7. Is your feeling more than personal attraction? Do you need his physical presence to be enthusiastic?
8. Do you like him as a person or do you like only a feeling about him? Is he attractive because of what he is or what you "read into him"?

All of which boils down to are you in love with love—or do you get beneath the shiny veneer that surrounds all engaged couples or sweethearts?—*Boston Post.*

PUT *Charm* IN YOUR LETTERS

by Margery Wilson
Condensed from CHARM

THOSE of us who wish to be more charming, that we may give and get more of the good things of life, must take advantage of every opportunity to make a pleasant and attractive record of ourselves. Through a proper understanding of the best uses of correspondence we can radiate our charm to absent friends, keep ourselves alive in the minds of those removed from us, lay foundations for future delightful times, heal misunderstandings, give great pleasure, and enjoy appreciation of all we have done.

Nothing is so gladly received as a good letter. For a letter is a flattering compliment of attention. Some one has thought of us. When we contribute to this happy experience we are going to be remembered pleasantly. We may write ourselves large on many hearts with the point of a pen.

We all whip our restless procrastinating selves into writing a certain number of duty letters, necessary messages. Comparatively few of us take full advantage of the possibility of the greater power and influence we may enjoy by writing those letters we do not have to write.

The greatest reason for this lack is that we are not prepared with the implements of writing, convenient enough to let us carry out an impulse to write some one a chatty letter before that urge has left us. The poorest room may have a rude desk or table with inexpensive appropriate stationery, stamps, ink, and pens.

A kindly, simple letter carries just as much thoughtfulness as the most brilliant epistle—so we should not hesitate to write letters, and lots of them, just because we do not write well.

And, too, if we become sufficiently interested in anything, sooner or later we will make it our business to find out how it is correctly done. Through practice we will develop a feeling for values and in a short time we will surprise even ourselves with our excellence.

Any kind of letter is better than none, except the sort that spends most of its space in apology of various kinds. On paper, in speech, anywhere, any time, apology should be very brief; not hurried and indifferent, but we must not hang over the matter and abase ourselves too much.

The use of the word "excuse" is a silly habit. If you have hurt some one physically or mentally, caused inconvenience accidentally or thoughtlessly, an excuse does nothing but lamely try to explain your own lack. It is weak. What do you want an excuse for? There isn't any to be had. Say what you mean, "I am so sorry," and let the matter drop.

If you are writing from some remote place where nothing is to be had but a pencil, don't go into a long stupid apology about it. You might say something like this, "I am writing to you with the only available tools, but so great is my desire to talk with you now that I would willingly scratch the words on tree bark with a nail," and go on with your letter.

Don't assume an exaggerated inferiority. Belittling ourselves is simply a bad habit.

In spite of all the jokes we hear relative to writing about the weather, it remains an always interesting subject. We are glad to know whether or not the winter in Florida has been pleasant, if our friends in the Middle West have had enough rain to suit them, if the Coast is too damp for older folks in whom we are interested.

Don't be afraid to talk about it. Remember that the spring has inspired our greatest poets to their highest flights of picturesque language, and all the other seasons have to be lived with.

Everybody knows that after enjoying some one's hospitality, it is necessary to write a letter expressing appreciation, so necessary that we call these obligatory messages "bread and butter" letters. There is a lovely girl who has made a practice of writing to her hostess twice after a visit. The first letter is expected, demanded by usage and cannot possibly carry the flattering idea of impulsive thought; so a day or two after she has mailed her bread and butter letter, she dashes off a little note about the lingering pleasure of something that occurred before she left. She often writes just a short little page, but as it is not a duty this second note is very personal and pleasing.

These things are no part of etiquette—we can get along very well with "bread and butter" letters; but impulsive little messages add to our charm. It is so much kinder to drop a clever little note to a busy acquaintance than to call him to the telephone, to listen to what you have on your mind.

Never use correspondence cards. They are ungraceful and ungracious, carrying with them the suggestion of a premeditated brevity.

We might neglect a letter of condolence indefinitely, if we saw only light gay stationery on our desks, but if we saw there a soft dove gray we would sit down immediately and write a letter of sympathy, for the subdued gray would suggest harmony with the subject-matter. And speaking of sympathy, let us make our letters of condolence short, very short— little more than a mental handclasp. We cannot fully experience another's sorrow and the cruelty of long wordy messages at such a time is known only to those who receive them. Some people seem literally to roll up their sleeves and settle down to the grim joy of cruelly stirring up the emotions of the bereaved, but all is neatly wrapped up in allusions to eternity and the beauties of the after-life, harrowing the feelings of the reader in an effort to comfort.

Brevity in a business letter is desirable and kind. Here the third person is entirely correct.

But when you write to your soldier, beware of brevity, beware of the third person. Fill your letter full of "you" and "I," full of news, warmth and cheerfulness.

Form the charming habit of writing notes of congratulation to your friends who are graduating, and in these happy messages you may spread yourself in all your literary splendor. Your thoughtfulness will be remembered an entire lifetime. Truly a bargain in charm. Write your thoughts to interested friends. It is a delightful form of self-expression and through it you may create a trail of graciousness, thoughtfulness and love that will enrich your life in many ways.

~~~~~~~~~~~~~~ ☀ ~~~~~~~~~~~~~~

Harness Your Wish

Angelo Patri

HIDDEN DOWN DEEP, so deep it has roots in your soul, you have a wish. If you hold fast to that wish, thinking it, living it, day after day, with all your heart and with all your soul, backed by the might of your intelligence, it must come true. You become your wish. Nothing, nobody, can prevent that.

There are always obstacles to be overcome, to call out your resistance. These are essential to your growth. Keep hoping; keep searching, and before long the world will be filled with opportunities, information and help. You will find it in the newspapers, the magazines, and books. You will meet people interested in your ideas, and consequently, in you, friendly people who will lend their strength to yours.

I once knew a girl who had a wish like that. She was then about ten years old. "When I am big I am going to live in a stone house, with a fireplace and a shiny copper kettle and a little dog. I am going to write a book."

The time came, some 30 years afterward, when she sat in that house by that fire, watching the flames dance on the shining kettle. At her feet lay the little dog, and in her hand she held the book. She had lived out her wish and it had brought her happiness, success, and best of all, the feeling of fulfillment.—*Youth Today.*

Vocational Friendship is a simple idea which will guarantee you a lifetime of pleasure

WHY WE LOSE OUR FRIENDS

by Gelett Burgess

WHEN I was young I was romantic. I believed in Santa Claus; I believed that all women were angels. And I believed in friends. But after years of discontent with Toms who bored me and Dicks who lied to me and Harrys who double-crossed me, not to speak of Janes who talked me to death, I was almost ready to exclaim with Job, "Have pity on me, O ye my friends!"

What was the trouble? Why is it that we're so often dissatisfied with our friends? Why are we shocked, disappointed or angry at their actions? Is it true, as Ralph Waldo Emerson said, "Friends such as we desire are dreams and fables." Not at all. I found out, in time, that the fault wasn't with Tom, Dick and Harry but with myself. For friendship is one of the most difficult games in the world.

It has to be understood and practised as scientifically as chemistry, parachute jumping or painting.

The secret lies in what I might call Vocational Friendship. The vocational expert, you know, is a person who goes to a big store or factory and examines all applicants for jobs, mentally and physically, to determine what each one is best suited for. Then he assigns them to the departments where they'll be most efficient. Sometimes a failure as bookkeeper will be a great success at washing windows; and a man who couldn't possibly run a machine will handle splendidly a whole herd of stenographers. So that's exactly what you must do to your friends to make them most worthwhile and permanent—understand and classify them and not attempt to make square pegs fit into round holes.

Now Arthur, for instance, is a witty and amusing talker. But he never keeps his appointments. So just enjoy his talk when you meet him, but don't make any appointments with him; then he'll always please you. Why curse Gertrude—who plays auction bridge like an Ely Culbertson just because she dresses like a frump? Have her for a partner when you play, but don't take her to a night club. Then you'll always be friends. For the purpose of display you can escort Elsie who is pretty—but dumb.

55

I had a cousin who exasperated me for years because she would never answer my letters or even acknowledge the receipt of gifts I sent her. But she has lovely table manners and can eat asparagus, oranges, frog's legs or even corn on the cob so that you are hardly aware of it. Well, what did I do? I gave up writing to her but whenever she was in town I took her out to dinner. We have been great friends.

You see, it is impossible to change people and make them what you like. But if you enjoy each one in the special way in which each excels you'll never be disappointed or irritated. The trouble is that most of us expect each of our friends to be like those many-bladed knives that boys love, knives that can cut, bore holes, drive screws, open cans and do almost anything. We expect friends to please us in everything.

But friends are like simpler tools. Each one can do something well, and we should use each one only for that. We can't complain, "You naughty screw driver! Why can't you drive nails?" so why should we expect a woman who can write wonderful poems to tell funny stories or do the Rumba? Can't a man play a marvelous game of golf and yet be careless about his debts?

Vocational friendship would teach you to use him only for golf and never lend him money.

The art of Vocational Friendship, you see, is to keep your contact with friends only to those points where you're mutually sympathetic. With some friends you may find many pleasant points of contact, with some only a few. But almost every person you meet has at least one quality that you can enjoy. That is the way I think that we should look at our friends. *Focus on the quality you like best.*

Anyway, I have found that in this way I could be friends with almost everybody. Not expecting more than one specialty of each, I was never disappointed in my friends.

YOUR VOICE

Wʜᴀᴛ a tattle-tale your voice can be! Don't let it tell things on you that are not true or reveal those things you would rather keep to yourself. Learn to listen to the sound of your own voice. Watch for pleasant tone, clear enunciation, and correct pronunciation. Voices can be magnetic or as irritating as squeaky chalk on a blackboard. Certainly an important ingredient in feminine charm is a soft, low-pitched voice. There is no greater aid to business, professional or social success than a pleasing voice and the knowledge of how to use it in interesting conversation. It helps to hob-nob with books on grammar. Keep on speaking terms with the rule. Don't be afraid of pronouncing your words as the dictionary tells you, but practice them so that they sound as if they really belonged to you and were not borrowed for the occasion.—Aʟʟᴇɴ ᴀɴᴅ Bʀɪɢɢs in *Behave Yourself*, published by Lippincott & Co.

$\mathcal{G}lamour$ $\mathcal{G}irls$ ARE MADE—NOT BORN

by Elizabeth Mather Young
Condensed from THE WOMAN

I KNOW YOU are becoming pretty impatient with articles on glamour. You're probably sitting here this minute with a laced-up corset and several books about charm on the nearest table. You've dramatized your appearance as far as the budget will permit. Your voice is a melody, your perfume a siren song, and your poise is the talk of three bridge clubs.

But the man in your life still calls you Toots. So you've decided that Hedy Lamarr can go her way and you'll go yours, and the articles on glamour will be nice to start the fire with, come winter.

The situation isn't as hopeless as it seems, though. It's not that you just aren't the type. Glamour is not peculiar to any one "type" of woman. Nor is it that everything you've read about acquiring glamour is the product of a fevered mind. Poise, becoming clothes, careful grooming, a pleasant voice, and a genuine interest in other people are all essential to a glamourous personality. Truly glamourous women possess all of these attributes. But they possess one more, one that has not been emphasized sufficiently.

The very foundation of glamour is the ability to be silent about your personal troubles and problems. Glamour is based on mystery and illusion, not on revelation. If you want to be glamourous, you must give the impression that your life, as well as your appearance, is flawless. Can you imagine the Duchess of Windsor discussing her makeup problems at a tea, or do you think for a moment that Lynn Fontanne entertains people with a graphic description of her last trip to the dentist? These two charming women have problems and troubles just like the rest of us, but they are smart enough to be quiet about them and to create the illusion that their lives are as unclouded as crystal.

A slim figure will help you give an impression of beauty and charm only if you refrain from telling everyone what you go through to keep that willowy silhouette. Otherwise people will think of you as doing bending exercises, instead of as a slender creature of mystery.

I met a beautiful and charming woman at a party the other evening. She was poised, graceful, immaculately groomed, her conversation stimulating. I would have carried away the impression of a glamourous woman if I had not met her in the dressing room at the end of the evening. She was standing before a mirror, fussing with her hair.

"You know, I've been just miserable all evening," she volunteered. "My regular girl was sick today, and a strange operator fixed my hair, and she didn't do it at all right. The curls should be up higher and I never have a wave at the left side like this."

Her words shattered the illusion of glamour. Suddenly she was only another woman who had to have her hair set for parties. I could see her sitting under a dryer, a net on her head, a towel around her shoulders, just one of the girls. Even Helen of Troy had to have an occasional shampoo, I'm sure, but you find no references to the fact in history.

Don't fill your conversation with domestic details. There is nothing romantic about the butcher, the baker, or that wonderful dressmaker you've found who makes divine fall suits out of old overcoats. You must relegate them to the back streets of your conversation if you want to be a *femme fatale*.

Censor your conversation at home as well as abroad. There is no point in barricading yourself behind closed doors during your face cream orgies, or in shopping madly for a dress that makes you like something Chanel might dream of, if you regale your husband with an account of the day's housecleaning chores. No man was ever swept off his feet by a woman's housekeeping ability. He may appreciate it. He may feel that it is an essential quality in a wife, that it is a vital part of a successful marriage. But it is not the stuff that dreams are made of.

You can't have everything, and in the long run it's more gratifying to be considered enchanting than capable. So the next time your husband compliments you on your appearance, don't tell him with pride that the dress you are wearing is something you whipped together from a remnant. Just smile your most ravishing smile, and let him think your attractiveness is the result of long hours spent among silken cushions dreaming of him.

Now that you know how it's done, I hope some unknown uncle dies and leaves you his cache. Buy a season ticket to the best beauty salon in town, order a closet full of bewitching clothes, and do what the charm books tell you. You'll be glamourous—if you don't tell people how you got that way.

It's Easy to Be Popular

by Marian W. Pease

DORIS: Oh, is that your new suit?

You: Yes. Do you like it?

Doris: It's smart—but *I* found a beauty! A lovely sheer wool, and it's a perfectly divine shade of green. Bob says it's the best-looking suit he's seen this season and it's the best I've seen!!

If you are eager to see Doris again soon after this chat and are happier about your new suit than you were before you met her, don't read any more.

There are 130 million Americans *selling* every day of their lives. About six million know they are selling, because their bread and butter depends upon it. What of the 124 million of us who are not selling refrigerators, automobiles or lace nightgowns? Do we spend time acquiring skill in salesmanship? No. We are selling, though, every day. We are selling ourselves.

Everyone who isn't a hermit is a salesman because selling is a social act. The reason a meeting between two or more people can never be neutral is that the one who has more to give and knows better how to give it is the better salesman. Selling is giving.

Ask the refrigerator salesman. He won't tell you he is selling enamel and steel. He will say: "Oh no. I talk up the benefits of modern refrigerators to my customers." A good insurance salesman is firmly entrenched behind the idea that he is giving protection, not selling policies. Do cosmetic manufacturers claim to sell so much of this and that? No. They would *give* you "the skin you love to touch."

The sale we make is the impression we give—a simple sale, but to us as important as if we got money for it. Our success or failure in this determines whether our relatives, associates and in-laws love us, are indifferent to us, or hate us.

Suppose one summer, both your daughters being out of town, you invite the sons-in-law to dinner one at a time. First comes Bill:

Bill: Terribly hot, isn't it?

You: Yes. Perhaps you would rather have stayed in town than take the trip out here?

Bill: It was pretty bad! The train was crowded and I had to stand all the way out. I didn't even have a chance to read my paper, so, if you don't mind I'll just sit here and look at it till dinner time. . . .

The following evening Tom arrives.

Tom: I'm certainly glad to be here. It's good to have a breath of fresh air! *You:* We do get a breeze here if there's one stirring . . . would you like to read your paper till dinner's ready?

Tom: I should say not! There must be something I can do. (He walks to the kitchen with you.) I see you've remembered my weakness for fried chicken, but it was a shame to struggle with it this hot night. I'm glad you did, though!

Which son-in-law are you going to invite more often?

Sometimes we speak of those people who get along so well with other people as if they had been born that way. The truth of the matter is that their success is based on one very simple formula. Here it is: *You can sell yourself to any normal human being (and most cats and dogs) by expressing your sincere interest in or admiration for something they have, or have done.*

Sounds easy, doesn't it? Take two grown-ups

with the opportunity of selling themselves to a child:

Grown-up 1: How do you do—let's see, what's your name?

Child: Jackie.

G.U. 1: Oh, yes, Jackie. I'd forgotten. It's been quite a while since we've seen each other, hasn't it? (Long pause. Then, looking wildly around): Where's your mother?

Jackie: Playing tennis.

Grown up says oh and leaves promptly for the tennis courts.

The second grown-up comes along:

Hellow, Jackie!—Say, it seems to me that dog of yours has grown since I saw him last. Have you taught him any new tricks?

Jackie: He can retrieve now!

G.U. 2: Can he? Well, isn't that something! Let's take him out in the backyard and see if he'll let you show him off.

Jackie: Sure.

And off they go like a couple of pals.

Which grown-up do you suppose Jackie likes better?

The formula holds true even though you meet someone for the first time. Perhaps you don't know anything about this man to whom

• *How easy it is to sell yourself! Shine up your admiration; put a new sparkle on your appreciativeness! You can sell yourself to any human being, simply by expressing your sincere interest in something they have done.*

you have just been introduced. You also don't know when you'll meet the person who will become the strongest influence in your life, so take no chances. Search instantly for anything interesting in him or in his background. If you find nothing, ask his opinion about something, indicating your sincere interest in his views. This split second may be the only opportunity you will ever have to sell yourself to him.

If it isn't, and the acquaintance ripens into friendship, you must keep this new friend sold on you in order to hold his friendship. You do this by continuing your interest in what he does for a living, what he has to say and think and do.

Fortunately, we don't have to learn a new formula for every meeting. Each time you see him you need only remember what interested your friend when you last met. Just always think about him and not about yourself. Forget *your* child. Ask about his. When he answers your questions, listen. Don't let him catch a faraway look in your eyes, because he will know at once that you're thinking about yourself, and promptly lose interest.

It's easy to see why some people sell themselves well and others do not. Notice the application of that simple formula by your son-in-law Tom and Grown-Up Number 2. And the neglect of it by your friend Doris, your son-in-law Bill and Grown-Up Number 1.

Are you convinced that the good salesmen were not born with the formula in their pockets? Personality is not like a silver spoon at all. It's more like an "open sesame" and everyone can learn its secret: You can sell yourself to normal men, women and children by expressing your sincere interest in or admiration for something they have, or have done. Whether we apply the formula or not is up to us.

※ ※ ※ ※ ※

Ten Rules for a Happy Marriage

1. Bear and forbear.

2. Work together, play together and grow together.

3. Avoid the little quarrels, and the big ones will take care of themselves.

4. Compromise. It is the antitoxin which destroys the poison eventuating in divorce.

5. Practice sympathy, good humor and mutual understanding, for they are the foundations of the perfect home.

6. Don't grouch before breakfast— or after it.

7. Respect your "in-laws," but don't criticise them nor take it.

8. Establish your own home, even in a one-room flat.

9. Fight for each other but not with each other.

10. Build your home on religious faith, and never let a day close without a clean slate of forgiveness.—JUDGE JOSEPH SABATH in *This Week*.

1

This is an exercise which furnishes the groundwork for the chassé and many popular variations. It is also the best exercise to use in training your toes to turn outward.

Place your feet together. Step backward with your right foot, then draw the left foot up to the right. Now step back again with your right foot and draw left foot up to the right foot again. Continue this routine, going backwards around the room. Remember that the toes must be turned out. Practice also with the left foot leading. Notice that when stepping backwards, the girl uses only the tips of her toes.

2

Many dancers who find the forward or backward steps easy to execute have difficulty with the side movements. This routine will improve your side-step, so important in many dances.

Rising on the toes of your right foot, raise your left foot as high as possible. Now lower the foot.

Repeat this exercise ten times with one foot, then repeat with the other. Count 1 - 2 - 3 - 4, as you practice, raising the foot as you count 1 - 2, lowering it as you count 3 - 4. Or practice to the music of your radio or phonograph.

FOUR EXERCISES

To Improve

3

This exercise will help you take long backward steps with free and easy grace—a most important thing for girls. Also, it will make you hold your head high, and take the stiffness out of your back.

Stand erect, with your hands at your sides and heels together. Then swing into the position shown here. Repeat ten times. Don't bring the feet together again until after the third beat. Practice this routine to Waltz tempo by counting 1 - 2 - 3. The teachers in your nearest Arthur Murray studio will gladly demonstrate these exercises.

4

Any girl who has tried waltzing forward, while her partner danced backward, knows that going toward her partner gave her an uncomfortable feeling. This exercise will help you to follow in forward movements. Without bending the body forward, raise your right foot until it is parallel with the floor. Stretch your toes out—not up.

To develop your dancing poise, hold your foot up for five seconds, then lower it slowly. Do it without music. Repeat ten times, then try it with your left foot.

Your Dancing Style.

I was an
UGLY DUCKLING

by Kathryn Murray

PEOPLE of my age often say: "I wish I could be a child again, don't you?" My answer is "No." I'd hate to live my childhood over again.

My mother was a very pretty woman. She had red hair, blue eyes and a beautiful complexion. I was a sallow, tiny, dark-haired child — always the smallest of the group—always the homeliest. My uncle affectionately called me "Monkey." How I hated him.

I adored beauty. My mother's dresser drawers, fragrant with sachet, heaped with lacy, silky things held me spellbound for hours. My own finery consisted of a pair of black-and-white spangled shawls, discarded, out-of-date remnants. I loved dressing up and playing "pretend" over and over again. My favorite day dream was of myself, dressed in a frilly white net dress, over a pink satin slip, with rosebud trimming running 'round and 'round. In it, still in dreams, I would pirouette and dance for a great audience that would clap and cheer.

My mother had good taste in clothes. She knew her little Kathryn's drawbacks and she dressed me in neat, crisp linens, calculated to swell out over my skin-and-bone build.

We had a goodhearted and loving girl living with us. Not exactly a maid or servant — more of a "mother's helper." She was so fond of me that I had beauty in her eyes. For Helen alone I would dance—no one else ever knew. Up in Helen's little bedroom, I would dance in bare feet, in my little white slip and she would tell me that I was much better than the girl at the Orpheum. Once—I can remember it so clearly—we were at the seashore in the summertime; I had my first sunburn of the season and my thin cheeks were a glowing sunkissed red. My parents walked in the room and Helen, with loving belief said: "There, doesn't she look just like Mary Pickford?" Though they loved me, my parents rocked with laughter.

Helen tried her best with her ugly duckling. She brushed my hair over her finger until it looked like the loops in Palmer penmanship. She would plead: "Just hold your head still until your curls dry." Once, in a desperate attempt, she brushed my corkscrews with sugar water to make them hold.

When it dried, my head was a stiff, flaky, grayish brush—and I was irresistible to flies.

My father was a clever newspaper man, but though quick-witted, he had no inkling of my childish yearnings. He would say: "Well, kiddo, when you were born, you sure were a homely little jigger . . . one look at you and I went out and took a strong drink. Don't you care, baby, beauty is only skin deep—we'll skin you and you'll be just fine." I used to laugh, the hearty pathetic laugh that is the defense of unhappiness and self-consciousness.

I suppose I was a fairly bright child. Teachers in the lower grades skipped me until my mother objected. I was ready for high school at eleven. High school! How I looked forward to it. How bravely I set forth every morning, swinging my lunch kit—complete with thermos. Those thermos bottles, so fragile, so unlucky in my hands. I never walked. I always dog-trotted or ran. I fell on curbs, stumbled up steps, rushing, dropping, breaking. To this day, my shins and knees are covered with dozens of scars.

High school! So many big boys—so many pretty girls—and I was always the smallest, thinnest and homeliest. I had one crush after another on some little male, complete in his sheepskin-lined mackinaw. For quite a while, no one even knew I existed. And then I learned what I've never forgotten. No matter what a little girl looks like, she can become almost anything she wants.

I was naturally warm-hearted and affectionate. I not only craved friends but I wanted them to be really fond of me, to admire me. I wanted desperately to be popular.

I determined to stop being background—to step forward and get a little attention. Popular girls, I had noticed, could do things—they were fun to be with. I put myself in tune by learning every new song that came out. I memorized the words of all the new and old hits. I learned to strum a ukulele. I practiced dancing by myself for hours. I became a good dancer and one of the most popular boys sought me out as a partner.

This new attention was all the spur I needed. I felt a new inner happiness and began to blossom out. I found that conversation with boys and girls was fun, almost a game. I remember planning "lines" and "planting" them. I maneuvered conversations until I could let forth one of my wisecracks. Fortunately, I didn't try to monopolize the chit-chat. It was easy for me to be a good listener because I was delighted and flattered when boys and girls talked to me. I liked people enough so that my interest in them was sincere . . . I enjoyed their remarks, their jokes and I let them know that I thought them clever.

I was so anxious for companionship that I unconsciously made a superhuman effort to please everyone. As a little girl I had no interest in baseball or football, but I learned enough about them to carry on a conversation with completely muscle-bound youths. And it came naturally to me to say: "You were wonderful in the game last Saturday."

It wasn't just toward the boys that I directed my attention—I wanted girl friends, too. If I thought a girl was pretty, I'd tell her so. If I thought she had fine taste, I'd ask her advice. You must understand that I didn't have a deep-dyed purpose behind all this. No, my sole desire was to have friends—I liked the boys and girls and wanted them to like me. I now realize that the quickest path to popularity is to like and appreciate others.

By the time I met Arthur Murray, I had the self-confidence that is the reward of those who overcome handicaps. Undoubtedly, it was those years of striving to make friends that had given me personality enough to be attractive to a man who had met so many beautiful, charming girls.

My first date with my husband was for dinner at a swank restaurant. We had plans to go to a theater but, lo and behold, it suddenly was 10 P.M. and we had missed most of the show. "Imagine," he said, "we have been talking for three hours. I feel as though we've only been together for a few minutes!" After we were engaged to be married, I asked: "What made you propose to me?" He said: "After our first date I kept thinking how much fun it would be to have a wife who was such good company." Now, how do you like that for a glorious compliment? I loved it! The funny part of it was that I didn't remember talking at all—I thought Arthur Murray was the attractive and fascinating one.

Now that I am older and I have more mature judgment, I can realize that those who must make a conscious effort to please others, always get back ten-fold in results. Look around at the beautiful girls you know. Isn't it true that most of them are not shining successes, in business or in private life? I believe it is because they have never had to exert themselves. They have taken admiration and attention for granted and have just relaxed.

So when I am asked: "Wouldn't you like to be a child again?" . . . I can truthfully say: "Oh no" . . . but I must admit that I'm glad I was that homely little chick who had to scratch and dig. The corn tasted sweeter that way!

Answers for "Embarrassing Moments"

1. "Say, Helen, I'm hungry. What do you have in the icebox?"

2. "Do you think she knows that Mr. Brown prefers to dictate to you?"

3. "You're quite right, dear. The house does have an unpleasant odor. Help me open the windows to air it out." Or, "How about having you smoke some of your aromatic pipe tobacco? That always has a pleasant odor."

4. "You're right, Ruth; my alumnae are here tonight. I know you won't want to stay but I've spoken to them about you and I want you to meet them; then I'll let you go."

Find out if you can adapt yourself equally to a quiet evening at home and a gay night out

Are you FUN to be with?

Condensed from EVERYBODY'S WEEKLY

IF YOU want to know how you rate as an all-around good companion, check up on your behavior in the following questionnaire. Perhaps the result will surprise you! It may even explain why husbands leave home! Score one for every "Yes" and a nice round zero for "No."

1. Do you think the expression "I'll try anything once" is an "unintelligent" rule for living?

2. Do you like to meet new people?

3. Can you spend an enjoyable evening at home occasionally with a book or with an elderly relative?

4. Do you dislike card parties?

5. Do you love dances where they hand out funny hats, whistles, balloons and noise-makers?

6. Do you like to wear hats that make people turn around for a second look?

7. Do you drink enough to get "giggly" when you are dating?

8. Do you ever turn on the radio or the phonograph and dance around or sing to its accompaniment, all by yourself, without feeling too silly?

9. Do you think that conversation to be amusing should bristle with the newest slang expressions?

10. Can you spend a pleasant evening at home with your date, or do you feel that the time is wasted unless you go out dancing or to the theater?

11. Do you like to join large parties, even though you are not especially fond of the people in them?

12. Are you constantly experimenting with your hair, your make-up, and fancy tones of nail polish?

13. Do you usually change into more festive attire in the evening on the slightest excuse?

•14. Do you enjoy hearing or retelling risqué stories?

15. Do you think that it is worthwhile sometimes to just "sit and listen"?

16. Do you keep up with the latest dance steps and think swing and the

67

rumba and the samba are "divine"?

17. Can you spend an evening with people much older or much younger than yourself without feeling bored or superior?

18. Do you get jittery if you have to spend considerable time on your own resources?

19. Do you change your "dates" regularly instead of sticking to one "tried and true"?

20. Do you indulge in practical jokes?

Add up your total. If it comes between 16 and 20, you are a touch *too* gay; better watch that you don't overdo. Between 10 and 15, you rate as a cheerful and restful companion, adaptable for any engagement. From 5 to 9, better watch your introvert tendencies. Below 5, snap out of your glooms! You're no fun at all.

Let Your Eyes Smile

A FEW YEARS ago the sales head of one of America's largest corporations assembled his sales force to meet Jay B. Iden, a New York stage director. Mr. Iden was to teach them to smile! He took them one by one, analyzed their smiles, criticized them. Many thought they knew how to smile, but Mr. Iden convinced them that they merely smirked. In a true smile, the eyes also smile. In a smirk, only the mouth smiles. The eyes may seem hard, unfriendly. After two weeks' training, the men went out of the smile clinic and in three months increased their sales 15 per cent. The best salesmen, the best actors, the most successful leaders of people have not been above rehearsing their little smiling act in privacy in front of the mirror.—*Think What You Want.*

You're a Good Conversationalist If You—

1. omit unnecessary details which lengthen a story.
2. await an answer to the question asked you.
3. don't ask personal questions.
4. ask questions that show you're interested.
5. don't interrupt.
6. make your story short unless you're a rare raconteur.
7. never argue when the subject is of minor importance.
8. like to hear the other person talk, too, and give him a chance.
9. talk about yourself without being known as an "I-Me-My" person.
10. are careful to keep to subjects of interest to all.
11. avoid subjects which might embarrass others.
12. listen well and interestedly.

—*Woman's Almanac.*

To have friends is insurance against loneliness. And the price of this insurance is very low!

There's a Knack in Making People Like You!

by Adele de Leeuw

IF YOU want people to like you, you must like them.

Liking people, first of all, must spring from your realization that they are human beings like yourself—with the same worries and tribulations, the same joys and expectations. Liking people doesn't mean you want to run their lives for them; it means that you realize they have lives of their own, and you respect their right to live them. If help is needed, you're willing to give it, but you know, too, that someday you may need help as much as they. Help is a big word. It covers a multitude of services.

Liking people makes you observant, understanding and tolerant. Because you have let your heart as well as your eyes and mind understand Mrs. Wong, you know she's a hard-working, gentle soul who's always in terror that what she's done won't meet with approval. Simply praise her, not with empty words but honestly, when she does something well, and you see her beam and blossom before your eyes. You understand

that because Jennie Hale is lonesome she is withdrawing more into her shell; so you invite her to tea with a few friends and draw her out. You don't agree with Don Fentriss at all on his half-cooked ideas on politics, so when you meet Don you forget that side of his nature and remember the other traits you admire. You are aware that little Mr. Epstein is silent and morose only because he has a talkative wife and never gets a chance to speak; so you start a conversation and let him talk. Listening to the spate of words coming over the dam and watching his face light up you know you've done him a world of good.

Because you like people you do Mrs. Littleton's marketing for her when her car's out-of-order. You stay with Fanny Morelli's children one afternoon a week so that Fanny herself can get away from her treadmill. You take some jars of home-made jelly to the Old Ladies' Home, and you don't just run in and out— you stay and exchange a dish of gossip with the lively old ladies, and they enjoy that even more than the jelly.

Because you like people you recognize in them the same kind of fascinating characters that you find all too rarely—in fiction. Here, among your friends and acquaintances, the groceryman, salesgirl, carpenter, you have the stuff of fiction and the stuff of life inextricably bound. The chicken-and-eggs woman may have calloused hands and a chapped face, but she has a fine earthy philosophy that is more of a tonic than a good book. You discover that the unapproachable, very grande-dame Mrs. Fitzhugh is withdrawn and haughty because she has led a tragic life more stirring than any novel, and that she is ready to melt at the first hint of understanding. No detective story can compare with the thrill of unearthing the truth about Witherspoon—that he lost his wife and three children in an epidemic, shot the doctor, served a prison term, made a fortune in oil, gave it to outfit a hospital *in the doctor's name* and is now raising bees and doing research on the side.

Life is full of satisfaction when you like people—*enough*. When you aren't really surprised to find that the postman has put three sons through college; that the dowdy Miss Jansen is a ministering angel to the neighborhood; that Mrs. Lucas, who has lately taken to talking and laughing too much, is suffering from an incurable disease and is keeping the knowledge from her family.

You understand how people act because you know their feelings. You like them because they have as many facets as a well-cut diamond, and they lend sparkle and depth to your life.

Liking people has its selfish side, too. It's insurance against old age and loneliness. If you actually care what happens to the people you know, just because you're warm and sympathetic and they're people like yourself, you'll never be lonely.

The words and smiles and interest you give so freely will come back to you, as if they truly were bread cast upon the waters. When you need friends you'll have them; when you need help it will come; when you want a shoulder to cry on or a handkerchief to dry your eyes with, or a hand under your elbow on a stormy road, it will be there.

To measure your chances for happiness, be honest with yourself: how much do you really like people?

Sending checks for the leper colony, the starving in China, the refugees in Europe is fine. But there's this warm, breathing life about you that deserves your *self*—your liking self. For after all, Humanity with a capital H is made up of individuals, each one of whom needs the tone of someone's voice, the flash of someone's eye, the pressure of someone's hand, to round out his own life and give him a little happiness.

I feel sorry for the man who says that, compared to individual human beings, he finds that he likes dogs. It's quite possible that even the dogs don't care about him very much.

Do You Have A Sense of Humor?

It's hard to be a good sport when practical jokers are at large. Can you pass this test?

by J. W. Wrightstone, Ph. D.

Are you a good sport? Can you be the "goat" and like it? Here's a chance to test your sense of humor and to include best friends and family.

Check the one item under each question that comes closest to describing what you believe would be your most typical reaction under the circumstances. Be sure to check yourself as you really are, not as you would like to be. Then, after you have checked a situation under each of the eight questions, turn to page 108. You'll be surprised—pleasantly, we hope!

I. *If I were with a gang who laughed when some one said in banter, "We all saw you purposely drop your handkerchief so the good-looking stranger would notice you":*

a. I'd pretend I didn't hear the remark.

b. I'd join with the others in the fun.

c. I'd probably feel hurt and leave them immediately.

d. I'd curtly tell them that jealousy prompted their petty wit.

e. I'd reply with some wisecrack like, "To the victor belong the spoils."

II. *When I am the "goat"—a toy mouse under my chair, salt poured by the prankster into my cup of coffee, or choose your own practical joke:*

a. I play up to the situation, providing all the possible entertainment.

b. I wait my chance and repay the "wise guys" in their own coin.

c. I show my displeasure or reprove them in some obvious way.

d. I ignore the incident and turn my attention to other matters.

e. I enjoy the situation as much as any of the jokesters.

III. *When some one in a group tells a joke or funny story about Pat and Mike that I've heard before:*

a. I try to act as delighted and appreciative as when I first heard it.

b. I smile wanly and say it's a good joke.

c. I stop the person in the middle of the joke with, "I've heard that one before."

d. I let the person tell the joke, but I look sour.

e. I laugh heartily and say, "That reminds me of a similar story."

IV. When the comedian on the stage has the audience in stitches by his crazy antics:

a. I wonder what the audience can see in his crazy acts and remarks.

b. I am as amused by the audience as by the comedian.

c. I join with the audience in its hearty merriment—laughing with the best of them.

d. I enjoy some of the humor—chuckling to myself.

e. I am usually fed up and leave the place.

V. When I am explaining the brave deed I performed and some one acidly remarks, "My heroine, how wonderful you are":

a. I feel embarrassed and irritated by the remark.

b. I reply, "Of course, but not nearly so wonderful as you would be."

c. I say, "Sorry, but you can't get my goat that way."

d. I thoroughly enjoy the situation and laugh at myself.

e. I disregard the interruption and proceed seriously with my story.

VI. When one of my friends "takes me off"—disclosing and imitating my unique, individual mannerisms—before

a crowd of people who all know me.

a. I join fully and sincerely in the spirit of fun.

b. I find it difficult to hide my hurt vanity and pride.

c. I say that the "take-off" is grand and that it is very entertaining.

d. I tend to show my resentment by some biting remark.

e. I always think such forms of humor are cheap and degrading.

VII. When I've taken that unintentional and harmless spill on the ice, wet pavement, stairs, or rug:

a. I understand the humor occasioned by such an incident.

b. I resent the fact some persons use another's misfortune for their fun.

c. I hide my hurt feelings under the cover of a laugh at myself.

d. I jocosely remark that I'll have to have the offending object removed from my path.

e. I am irritated at my own clumsiness and spill a few tears.

VIII. When the party grows dull and drags along monotonously:

a. I grow dull and monotonous with the party.

b. I'm the so-called life of the party who tries to think of things to do to pep it up.

c. I try to aid and abet anyone in providing impromptu wit.

d. I try to stimulate some of the amateur wits to do their stuff.

e. I accept the course of events, doing nothing about it.

SOME FOLK *seem to git the idea they're worth a lot of money just because they have it.*—SETH PARKER.

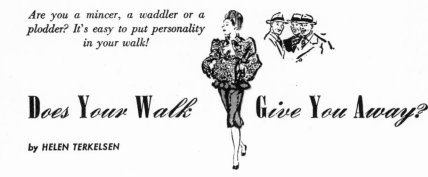

Are you a mincer, a waddler or a plodder? It's easy to put personality in your walk!

Does Your Walk Give You Away?

by HELEN TERKELSEN

DID YOU EVER stop to think of the personality angle of this walking business? Think of the people you pass daily on the street. Don't you have a definite impression of them from their method of locomotion? I'll bet you do, and don't forget that their eyes are not closed to your perambulations, either.

The truth is that the words which describe a woman's walk go far toward presenting a picture of her personality. That's how important the walking posture is.

Take the *mincer*. She might be described as a hothouse flower. Now I'm not implying, if you mince, that you hold your teacup with your little finger waving in the air. But mincing is a throwback to the day when women were bound by convention and corsets. They are bound by these things no more, so they shouldn't mince.

The first step toward curing the mince is to relax in every joint and muscle. Now swing the limbs freely while holding the torso still but not rigid. Set two chairs back to back about three or four feet apart and standing between them put one hand firmly on the back of each chair for support.

Stand on tiptoe and swing the left leg back and forth, pendulum fashion from the hip, with the knee joint absolutely relaxed. You will notice that there is another independent swing from the knee down. Doing the same with the right leg, you'll actually feel the loosening up of tight hip and leg muscles.

As soon as you realize how limber those legs were meant to be, try walking with that same freedom. At first it is better to exaggerate the flexibility and length of stride, and once that swing is attained, *control* it, don't *restrain* it, until the length of step is in graceful proportion to the length of the leg. The mincing is gone!

Long heavy strides, on the other hand, belong to the girl who is determined about whatever she does. She bears down in her scrubbing, her ironing, and even in her writing.

She's the one who practically pushes through the floor with every step. It's all right to step hard when leaving footprints for posterity, but for an everyday performance, no. It all tends to make her old ahead of her years.

Both the *bearer-downer* and the *plodder* have the same problem to overcome and by the same methods can do it. Instead of feeling themselves to be arrows pointing into the ground, they should imagine they are arrows pointing skyward.

If you have such a fault, try pushing your head up as far as possible (set a book on top of your head and see how much you can raise it), keep the shoulders back, but do not attempt to raise them except as they go with the entire body. Now walk across the room, still straining to make that book reach the ceiling and swinging your legs freely. See? There's no more bearing down, no plodding.

Almost in the same class are women who go through their twenties and thirties with heads bowed, and wake up in their forties to the realization that they were bowing to the inevitable—a dowager's hump on the back where the neck and shoulders meet. The book-pushing trick, if done consistently, will remedy that tendency in jig time.

We've all heard the comments when a *waddler* goes by. No matter how cute she may be, she completely deglamourizes herself with her duck walk. The whole trouble here is that she doesn't keep her feet parallel to the imaginary chalk line along which she walks, but swings in her heels instead with every step. This is why her cherub posterior wags from side to side. She also tries to straddle the whole sidewalk. The minute she starts keeping her feet straight ahead and in parallel lines not more than an inch apart, she'll lose the waddle.

If people say of you, "Poor old Minnie, she ain't what she used to be," you'd better check up on your gait.

Perhaps sore feet are preventing you from having a graceful walk; go to a chiropodist, of course, or stop wearing those ill-fitting shoes that look so beguiling when you sit down.

Affectation is a big source of a bad walk. You'll notice that children from four or five on seldom walk awkwardly, mainly because they haven't yet developed inhibitions or affectations.

Don't be affected. Do pull up to your fullest height. Do keep the weight over the ball of the foot. Do make sure that your joints—knees, hips or shoulders—are not locked. Do point your toes straight ahead, the feet in parallel lines about an inch apart.

That's all there is to it, and if you don't believe it's true, try it. Remember, a woman's walk can be as fascinating as her profile, her hair-do, and her voice,—or just as stridently unbecoming and unfeminine.

*Palm reading is surprisingly simple; try it! You'll have the
time of your life—and so will your friends*

TO BE POPULAR AT PARTIES—Read Palms!

by Marguerite Barze   Condensed from COLLEGE HUMOR

OPEN YOUR FINGERS, and let me see
what's in your hands!

"Nothing," you say. But you are
wrong! The story of your heritage,
the history of your life is contained
in the palms of the hands. And the
size of the hands, the shape of the
fingers, and the way they are set
upon the hands, reveal
your characteristics,
your type.

Open them out nat-
urally. Do you spread
the fingers apart, with
widely separated spaces
between? Then you are
unconventional, inde-
pendent.

Maybe your fingers
curve quite a bit. You are secretive,
reticent, do not want people prying
into your business. Now, isn't that so?

Does your thumb jut out stiffly;
is it strong and straight? This shows
courage, physical and mental. If the
tip curves distinctly down, you are
original and daring. This type of
thumb is invariably found in the
artistic hand.

Do your two middle fingers cling
together more than the others? That
shows barriers of restraint or convention you cannot break down. Is your
little finger very short? Your judgment is not of the best. Is it crooked?
Sh-h, you may be dishonest—provided you have not bent it by accident at some time or other. Are the
joints heavy? Well, don't get mad,
but that denotes
temper!

Now turn them over.
Do the fingers look
much longer from the
back than from the
palm side? That means
you consciously or un-
consciously give others
a wrong impression of
yourself.

Do your nails break easily? Versatility is yours. Are they blue or
purplish? Bad circulation, that's all.
And if they are ridged, you are un-
dernourished and need a tonic!

And those lines in the hand—what
has made them? Usage, of course!
We unconsciously move our hands in
a manner expressive of our activities,
our natures, our work, our play. The
lines change as we grow and develop,
especially those in the right hand if

you are right-handed and those in the left hand if you are a south-paw.

And no two hands are alike. In fact, your own hands are quite unlike each other. The left discloses hereditary tendencies; the right, growth of personality.

Most of us have mixed hands: a combination of three main types. But every hand inclines more to one type than to the other two, and that is the type governing the interpretation of what your hands reveal.

The *artistic* hand is long-fingered, flexible, with tapering fingers and moderately square palm. The skin is fine, given to many little lines, with well-defined major lines. The possessors of such hands are not always artistically gifted, but are *influenced* by artistic things—color, harmony, rhythm. A very narrow palm points to visionary qualities and indicates the idealist, ruled more by the heart, however, than by the head.

Two other main types of hands are (1) the *business* or practical hand, with short fingers, square palm, large mounts and fewer lines, the hand itself less flexible; and (2) the *coarse* hand, which has stubby fingers, thick short palm, heavy skin, sparse lines that are red and short, and short heavy nails.

Short fingers on the *practical* hand may be very tapered, showing a fine combination of the *artistic* and *practical*.

The line running around the thumb is known as the line of *Life;* the one crossing the palm below the little finger toward the fourth finger, the line of *Heart*. The one below it, running more or less parallel to it, is the line of *Head;* and the one extending from the base of the palm up through the center of the hand, the line of *Fate* or *Destiny*.

The most important line is the *Heart* line. It helps interpret all the others. It stands for affections, friends, love interests, maternal or paternal instincts—all human contacts. If it is long and clean-cut, moderate in color and width, unbroken and branched, it is an excellent *Heart* line. *Heart* lines with little lines branching from them mean many heart contacts.

Head lines stand for intelligence, brain activity, and all phases of mental life. They begin somewhere between the thumb and forefinger, and run in the opposite direction to the *Heart* line, but somewhat parallel to it. If the *Head* line is very straight, and crosses the whole hand, it shows that one is critical and probably literary. If it slopes to the mount of imagination, the cushion of the palm well below the little finger, it indicates imaginative tendencies.

The *Life* line stands for health and vigor. An island means illness, a break means accident or shock. Some hands have a second, or protective, *vitality* line, inside the *Life* line, which is security from health misfortunes.

The *Fate* line deals with destiny and material welfare. Breaks often mean change of occupation, moves, new decisions. Sometimes this line is stopped by the *Head* line, sometimes by the *Heart* line, but occasionally it crosses both and climbs high up in the hand. This means a clear-cut destiny, probably an outstanding one, which nothing can deter.

The circular line running from between the first and second fingers and circling around between the third and fourth fingers is the *Girdle of Venus*, and shows personal magnetism, high emotionalism, possibly Bohemianism.

Often a second line, known as the line of *Personality*, or *Fortune*, runs alongside the *Fate* line. This increases the strength of the *Destiny* line, and is a good sign. *Stars* on lines or mounts mean unusually successful achievements; crosses mean much the same thing.

Mounts are the little cushiony bumps below the fingers, at the base of the thumb and on the opposite side of the palm. The one below the first or index finger shows degree of ambition, or ego; the one below the second finger, material success; below the third finger, art; and below the fourth, gaiety and affection. The cushion at the base of the thumb stands for affection, and if quite high and bulging, points to possessiveness, perhaps jealousy. The one opposite it is the *Imagination* mount, and indicates intuition, visualization, possibly inventiveness.

Little fine lines running from the *Life* line at right-angles across the thumb stand for worries. The wider apart they are, the less one is prone to fret over little things. The lines or brackets around the wrist stand for physical vitality and magnetism. And, naturally, with all mounts, the higher they bulge up the more dominant is the quality for which they stand.

The finger joints. If the length of bone between the first and second joints is quite long, it shows emotionalism—even wilfullness, if much longer than the bone section between the second and third joints, which stands for reasoning and cool calculation. If the middle joint on the thumb is longer, it shows will power to a marked degree, and can easily lengthen into stubbornness.

The index finger is the finger of authority. If it is long and strong with a full base, you are a leader in thought and action. If long and thin, you are idealistic. If it is short, it denotes a lack of creative ideas, but a love of nature and outdoors. The index finger is usually a trifle shorter than the ring finger, but the loveliest hands have index fingers that are longer than ring fingers.

A star on the tip of your little finger is the *Star of Eloquence*. A *Star of Leadership* is seen in the hands of many great men, on the mount of ambition at the base of the index finger.

Fascinating, isn't it?

Your friends will be fascinated, too, when they find you can analyze their personalities by examining their hands.

How to Attract the Stag Line

By Mrs. Arthur Murray

Seventy-four men at the world's largest dancing school give their frank and surprising opinions on what they like—and dislike—about the way women dress. You can learn a lot, and win much pleasure, profit and popularity!

I INTERVIEWED 74 men at the largest dancing school in the world to find out what men like or dislike about the way women dress. I was amazed at the amount they know about women's clothes. And from now on, I'll take a man's say-so any time on how to dress for dancing.

What do you look at when you buy a dress for parties? Probably the front view. But when you wear it, it's the rear that comes in for attention. From the stag line at least. And your whole evening depends on whether they approve of how you look or not.

The men I spoke to all mentioned wide skirts immediately. They seem to like not only the flutter of a whirling skirt, but the way your legs are able to move *under* it. One man teacher told me that monthly dancing contests are held among the pupils at the studio. The winner among the women is not always the best dancer but is always the woman who wears a flared skirt that flatters her legs and feet and makes her steps look twice as dainty and graceful.

Try it yourself. Put on a narrow, bias, slinky dress and look in the mirror. From the front you may like the view and feel that you look as glamorous and seductive as a movie star. But look at the back and gaze at your figure in profile. The dress cups in under your sit-down, giving it more prominence than you deserve. And how about action? Try to step backward; stretching from the hip in a graceful, unbroken line. Try to do it! You can hobble, but you can't glide.

Now put on a full skirt. You can stretch back twice as far. You can reach 'way back to keep in step with the tallest partner and still look lithe and graceful.

When buying a special dress, pivot around and try to catch a glimpse of yourself in the mirror. If the skirt doesn't float or ripple as you turn, it's no eye-catcher . . . and it won't be flattering in motion.

Look over your shoulder and read your future from what you see. Raise your arms to your average partner's height to see whether your dress can take a dancing position—or whether it will shrug up too much.

With real evening dresses—the long ones—you don't have to sweep the floor for dignity and effect. The skirts can be a full inch off the floor and still look long and flowing. Every man has a horror of those too-long skirts that nestle right under his foot. Take the corté step, for instance. That's the little pet that has been nationally popular for many years. It's the one in which a man steps backward on his left foot, you go forward on your right foot, then dip. Try that step when you're deciding on skirt length. If inches of the skirt lie on the ground, shorten it. Or a man's foot may.

I spoke to men who are experts on the causes of poor dancing. Several of them told me that girls who ordinarily follow well often become difficult to lead when they wear the wrong shoes. Opera pumps, for instance, tend to slip off the heel on a backward step. Therefore, you tense your foot to hang on to the slippers and your dancing suffers. A T-strap or ankle-banded sandal is better for dancing—it will hold securely and you can forget your feet. Besides, the sandal type makes your feet look smaller.

The golden rule on dressing for dancing seems to be: "Look and feel right to your partner." And don't snicker at the "feel." A man's arm *does* encircle your frame, and a good dancer, with his weight carried forward, uses a certain amount of close-position chest lead.

If a taffeta or metallic dress feels stiff or dank or scratchy, say nay, nay to the salesgirl. There are enough soft, smooth fabrics which are pleasant to the touch.

Another touching subject: If you're a healthy animal and you perspire a bit after exercise, select dresses made of more absorbent fabrics, such as crepes.

Head lines are next in importance to the men. Soft, fluffy hair aureoled about your head is lovely in a photograph. But not so good in action. The young infatuated bridegroom who found a hair in his soup was not in the least mollified by his bride's "But, darling, it's *my* hair!"

Hair lines are important, but must be kept in line. A very small amount of a good, lightly perfumed lotion or brilliantine and a lot of brushing will keep your hair neat and tidy for the whole evening. Men seem to be terribly annoyed by girls who have to primp between dances.

When I say "lightly perfumed" for hair lotion, it's because men are so hard to suit. They spend hours at Christmas time sniffing dozens of bottles before they buy. You are safe if you use even the best perfume sparingly. No matter how light your touch is, the heat of the dance room will intensify the odor. And any man would prefer to think that a pleasant aroma is nine-tenths girl and one-tenth perfumer's invention.

With one accord the men pleaded against lipstick. Not on you, but on them! No man can think kindly of a girl who has thoroughly messed his appearance by a red smear on his tie, shirt or good gray suit. If you find an indelible lipstick, swear by it. In any case, be a little careful of how you turn your head.

If you're fond of a white or suntan makeup for your face and arms, experiment until you find one that doesn't rub off. You'll never make your mark in the world by leaving telltale traces of your complexion on a man's clothing.

Many dresses are trimmed by a huge gob of hard, bristly, artificial posies placed at the neckline or on the bosom. They give a pouter-pigeon effect and men loathe them. A girl instinctively draws back to protect her misplaced bouquet and feels like a wooden doll partner. Substitute soft chiffon flowers if you need trimming.

This front ornamentation of a dress goes for large buttons and buckles, too. The men are appalled by huge buckles with curlicues that catch in vest buttons. A girl's main object when dancing is to stay as light as thistle down. And her floating power vanishes when she has a cumbersome plaque of metal between herself and her partner's lead.

The men felt more than a little delicate about the next point I brought up. In fact, I had dozens of blushing males on my hands. It all started with a simple question about girdles. After much hemming and hawing, I pinned them down to facts. A girl might as well have a wooden leg as wear a girdle that is too long and tight for her.

Sacrifice a bit of line for comfort. Length in a girdle absolutely prevents freedom of motion. Tightness doesn't produce the desired slim effect anyway. It just pushes the plumpness into a ridge and makes it more noticeable. Your full skirts will cover figure deficiencies, so wear a foundation garment that stretches and one that has the added advantage of staying put. One man told me that nothing destroys illusion so much as the great American gesture (so he called it) of tugging down in the rear at a hidden undergarment.

While we were still on the subject of undergarments (it turned out to be pretty fascinating), one man mentioned the girls who allow slip and bra straps to show. This is extremely bad from the male viewpoint. It looks unforgivably sloppy—and of course it's so unnecessary. All you need to do is to sew little lingerie clasps in the shoulders of your dresses . . . you can buy the clasps in any dime store.

You shouldn't need a warning from men about how you look when your slip shows! Even complete strangers feel impelled to stop and tell you when that happens. As you test a dress for action by lifting your arms you can test your slip length at the same time. And don't forget that a dark slip is handy and dandy under a dark dress.

Every autumn, newspaper and magazine fashions alike come out with the "news" that black leads all colors for new clothes. This is no news to the men. They've always given black first choice. And the

Remember — when you dance —it's the rear view that comes in for attention

group of men I spoke to unanimously voted for black.

On second choice, it was a matter of individual taste. Red and blue were the most popular colors. Then turquoise, gray (surprising!) and beige. Green had four votes, yellow three, and the old favorite, pink, wasn't mentioned at all.

Now don't forget that this is not the latest from Mainbocher or Adrian. It's the opinion of seventy-four men in New York City who teach dancing daily to some of the smartest dressed women in town. They may not know about riding, golf or tennis togs, but they do know how a girl should dress for dancing.

॥॥॥॥॥॥॥ ✵ ॥॥॥॥॥॥॥

Do You Keep Your Friends?

How SUCCESSFUL are you with your friends? This questionnaire will tell you. To score yourself, count ten points for each question to which you can answer "yes" immediately. If you think a little before answering "yes," then count only six. When in doubt, count four points. A definite "no" gets a o. A score of 60 is bad; 86 means your friendships won't last long; 110 or more, a friend can rely on you for life.

1. Would you lend your best friend your favorite evening frock, if she needed it urgently?

2. Are you happy to receive a letter from your friend on a holiday, telling you what a wonderful time she is having—even though you weren't able to take a holiday yourself?

3. If your friend was broke would you lend her your best jewelry to pawn?

4. If you discovered a cheap smart dressmaker would you tell your friend the address?

5. Would you refuse to join in gossip about your friend?

6. Do you always offer your friend a cigarette when you have one?

7. Do you willingly agree to see a film or a play your friend wishes to see, even though you prefer a different one?

8. Would you stay up all night to nurse a sick friend?

9. When you go away, do you always write to your friends?

10. Supposing you disliked your friend's new dress, would you avoid criticizing?

11. Your friend's family is suddenly called away. Do you immediately ask, "Come round and have your meals with us"?

12. Would you refuse to steal your friend's beau?

—Everybody's

THE SWING STEP

A Fox Trot combination that expresses the feeling of blues music. This step is one of New York's most popular.

MAN'S PART

1. Side step to left.
2. Draw right foot up to left.
3. Side step to left—pause for a half second with weight on left.
4. Bring right foot up to left (no weight on right).
5. Step to right side on right.
6. Bring left foot up to right (no weight on left).

GIRL'S PART

1. Side step to right.
2. Draw left foot up to right.
3. Side step to right—pause for a half second with weight on right.
4. Bring left foot up to right (no weight on left).
5.. Step to left side on left.
6. Bring right foot up to left (no weight on right).

The Waltz is one of the oldest and most beautiful dances

The Waltz

THE WALTZ is one of the most beautiful dances of today and one of the oldest. Originated in Italy four centuries ago as a round dance known as a Volte, it spread to France and from there into other parts of the world. It has passed through many strange stages, many of which are hardly recognizable as the Waltz we know today. After the Hesitation (Waltz) appeared, the Waltz as it is known today, developed. Incredible as it may seem to a beginner, the Waltz step is actually the basis for most of the Fox Trot combinations.

Even though you have danced the Waltz before, study the following pages to be sure you are doing it correctly.

Don't merely memorize the steps—really learn *how* to do them. Each movement should be practiced over and over again until you can do it without having to think about your feet. When dancing to fast Waltz music with a partner, and changing from one direction to the other, you should not have to think about working out the steps—*know them*. These four steps comprise the Waltz as it is danced today.

1. **Forward Waltz movement.**
2. **Backward Waltz movement.**
3. **Left (reverse) Waltz turn.**
4. **Right Waltz turn.**

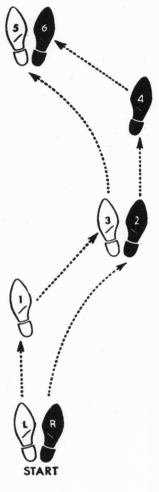

START

How to Waltz

FORWARD . . .

● Here is the count for the complete forward Waltz step.

1. Step forward on left foot.
2. Step diagonally forward to right.
3. Draw left up to right, weight on left.
4. Step directly forward with right.
5. Left foot to upper left-hand corner.
6. Draw right foot up to left, weight on right.

Practice this step for thirty minutes going around the room.

Hum or whistle with the music and then simply count ONE-two-three; FOUR-five-six. Accentuate the first beat by counting it louder.

Practice the forward Waltz one hour.

AND BACKWARD

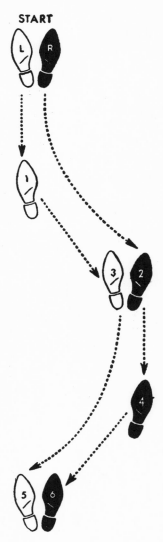

● The backward Waltz steps are just the opposite of the forward Waltz steps.

1. Step backward with the left foot.
2. Step back slightly to right with right foot.
3. Draw the left foot up to right, weight on left.
4. Step directly backward with right foot.
5. Step back slightly to left with left.
6. Draw right foot up to left, weight on right.

Practice the backward Waltz steps around the room. Start with the left foot backward.

Gradually do the movement faster and faster. Practice an hour to acquire ease and grace. After learning to Waltz forward and backward, try waltzing in both directions; first forward, then backward.

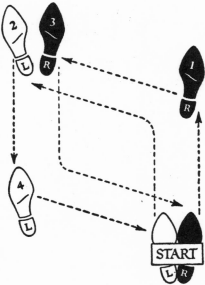

Note to Girls — Use the Man's footprints in learning the general pattern of this step.

Box Step
for the Right Waltz Turn

Lay out footprints on floor in accordance with diagram above.

1. Step directly forward with the right foot.
2. Left foot diagonally across square to upper left-hand corner.
3. Draw right foot up to left, raise left foot from the floor.
4. Step directly backward with the left foot.
5. Right foot to lower right-hand corner.
6. Draw left foot up to right, raise right foot from the floor.

The Box Step is the basis of the right Waltz turn.

The Right Waltz Turn

Arrange your footsteps on the floor in accordance with the diagram given below. Be careful to place footprints at the proper angle.

The right Waltz turn is exactly the same as the Box Step except that you turn to the right a quarter on the *first* of every three steps.

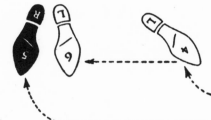

1. Step forward on right foot and at the same time turn body one quarter to right.
2. Place left foot forward to the side of right foot (feet apart).
3. Bring right foot up to left, raise left foot from floor. This completes a quarter turn.
4. Step directly backward with left foot, at the same time turning one quarter to right.
5. Place right foot to the side of left (feet apart).
6. Draw left foot up to right, raise right foot from floor.

The Left Waltz Turn

Arrange your footprints on the floor in accordance with the diagram given below.

Don't place footprints too far apart!

Don't place *any* footprint until you have first taken a long, but comfortable, step in the direction of that footprint.

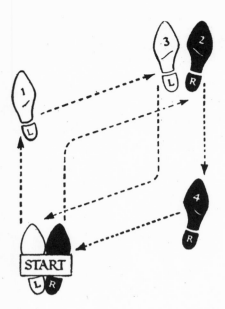

Note—Compare each step of diagram with description below.

Check each step in the diagram with the corresponding number in the instructions.

Box Step for the Left Waltz Turn

When doing the turns you do not have time to think of your steps; you must think of your direction, and the steps must be done almost mechanically. Therefore it is essential to *master* this Box Step which acts as the basis for the turn to the left.

1. **Step directly forward with left foot.**
2. **Side step to right on right foot.**
3. **Close left up to right and raise right foot from floor.**

This completes one Waltz step.

4. **Step straight back with right foot.**
5. **Left foot to the lower left-hand corner.**
6. **Close right foot up to left foot, raise left foot from the floor. (You then end up just where you started.)**

Repeat the six counts of the above movement until you can do it easily and rapidly.

THE MAGIC RHYTHM IN THE

FOX TROT

I CALL this the Magic rhythm because of its magical quality to change itself into any one of over thirty other steps. The rhythm of the magic step (2 slow and 2 quick steps) may be used in numerous variations.

After learning the magic step you will find that other steps are easy to learn and that you will be able to make up your own combinations of this interesting step.

MAN'S PART

Start with heels together.

1. Slowly walk forward with left foot.
2. Walk slowly forward with right foot.
3. Step to left side with left foot quickly.
4. Draw right foot up to left.

Note that the first two steps are done slowly; the last two are taken quickly. The rhythm is 1—slow, 2—slow, 3—quick, 4—quick.

For the Man

IF I WERE asked to tell the first secret of being a good leader, I would answer without hesitation: "A good leader is always *sure of what he is doing.*" If you are not sure of yourself, how can you expect your partner to be able to follow you? You must have your partner's confidence. *If your dancing convinces her that you know what you are doing, she gives you her confidence.* She will follow you readily if she has faith in your ability.

So I repeat: KNOW THE STEPS.

Secret of LEADING...

The mistaken idea that a Man should guide by pushing and pulling seems to live on, like a hardy perennial. Quite the contrary is true. The good dancer never thinks about leading his partner. *He merely does his own part well.*

Sometimes, when dancing with a partner who can dance well but is not yet familiar with the steps you prefer, you may have to do a bit of guiding. Then you indicate direction to your partner with your *right* hand and arm. Your right hand should be held firmly just above the Girl's waist. The left hand helps very little in leading.

In any case, the *beginner* is advised against forcible leading, for only advanced and intricate steps call for a strong helping hand. *You do not have to count or tell your partner what you intend to do next.* When dancing with a partner for the first time, start off with very simple steps. Introduce the more advanced steps gradually.

WHICH IS A RIGHT TURN AND WHICH IS A LEFT?

This is a question that is confusing to a beginner. To help you recognize the two turns quickly, here are two aids to turning in the proper direction:

1. To make a *right* turn, look over your *right* shoulder and let the rest of your body follow.
2. To make a *left* turn, look over your *left* shoulder and let the rest of your body follow.
3. To make a *right* turn, move the left hand *forward*. To make a *left* turn, move the left hand *backward*.

..AND FOLLOWING

for the Girl

AFTER dancing with women who boast that they can follow anyone I usually find they can follow only if I do steps with which they are familiar. I try new steps which they have never done and they are all at sea—as if they had never danced before. *The very first essential to successful following is:*

KNOW THE BASIC STEPS AND
THEIR POSSIBLE COMBINATIONS

You cannot expect to dance well with a man unless you are familiar with the steps he may do.

Always step in such a way as *always to be ready for the next step.* Develop a long, free, swinging step by making your toes go back as far as you can. Whether you go backward, forward, or sideways, dance as though you didn't have a foot *but only a big toe.* MAKE YOUR TOES LEAD. Dancing on the toes will help make you lighter. The exercises on pages 62-63 will help you tone up and make alert the muscles of your body which will respond instantly to your partner's leading.

To follow well, relax—do not bear down on your partner's arms. Many girls who are otherwise good dancers seem heavy when they allow their arms to sag. This is not relaxing. Practice dancing alone with arms outstretched at shoulder height *until your arms stay up without effort.*

Take the feet completely off the floor—do not slide them—when your foot is off the floor it is *ready* for the next step into which your partner leads you. Let your partner guide you through *his* movements—don't *fight* his leading. Don't think of *your* feet or steps—practice them until you can trust your feet and not your mind, to follow your partner. The lessons in this book are designed to train your *feet to remember the steps.* If you merely memorize the steps and do not *teach your feet by practice*, you will always be conscious of your steps and unconsciously interfere with your partner's leading.

HOW IS THE GIRL TO KNOW WHAT
HER PARTNER IS GOING TO DO NEXT?

If you have never danced with a partner this is the *most* mystifying question. Though her partner tries many variations of steps a girl will follow him readily if through practice she has developed a proper sense of dance rhythm. *Remember* that if you have learned your part of the *steps* you will know instinctively *what comes next*.

THE BILTMORE

an Advanced Waltz Variation

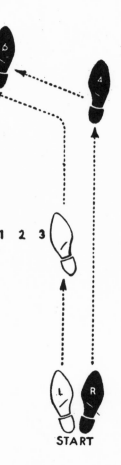

THIS is a favorite step of good dancers. It consists of a slow hesitation or balance step, followed by a quick waltz. (4, 5, 6.)

With left foot take a short slow step directly forward.

Hold the weight on that foot for three beats of the music. Count 1, 2, 3.

Then do a forward Waltz movement, begining with the right foot: 4, 5, 6.

To repeat, step forward with left foot.

The girl should learn the man's part first.

When doing her own part she begins with the right foot and goes backward.

Do you want to forget such ogres as timidity, fear or worry? You can. Here are ten tested techniques used by psychologists and doctors to help you forget

DO YOU WANT

A Better Disposition?

by Doron K. Antrim ❀ ❀ ❀ Condensed from THIS WEEK

AT WESTERN MICHIGAN COLLEGE in Kalamazoo, stutterers in the speech clinic of Dr. Charles Van Riper are being cured—by stuttering. In movies, drugstores, before any group of people who will listen, they try to stutter. In doing it deliberately, they gradually learn to control their speech and eventually to talk normally.

It's one of the new, successful techniques of forgetting used by psychologists and doctors. The sheer will power, do-or-die method of breaking a bad habit is less effective, since it takes no account of the unconscious mind—which invariably remembers when the conscious mind forgets.

Most of us would like to forget such ogres as timidity, fear, worry. You can. Just select the procedure that fits and give it a try. Here are ten tested recipes.

1. *Forget the thing you fear by doing it!*

Nerve-shattered blitz victims in England were treated to daily doses of bombing noises, recorded by phonograph. Their first reactions were far from encouraging. But after two weeks with constant repetition of "this is the kind that won't hurt you," patients took it without batting an eye.

A women afraid of cats was prevailed on to get a kitten as a pet. By the time it grew up, her fear seemed utterly ridiculous.

2. *Forget your fear by associating a pleasant thought with it.*

A two-year-old was terrified at his father's golf bag because it had fallen with a loud clatter. Each day his father placed a new toy nearer the bag, finally right on it. The boy's fear of the bag vanished.

A woman was afraid to go into the basement. She was told to take an absorbing novel and her dog to the basement and read for short periods. Gradually she lengthened the periods. In three weeks her bugaboo had gone.

3. *Consciously perform objectionable habits; you'll soon forget them.*

For nail biting—stand before the mirror five times a day, five minutes each time, and bite your nails. It takes only a few days to rid yourself of this habit.

4. *If a bad habit is pleasurable, you can forget it by making it unpleasant, difficult.*

Say you want to quit smoking. Instead of breaking off sharply, psychologist Henry Link tapered off. He carried no cigarettes at first and had to walk to a container for one, or beg from a friend. Next he stopped carrying matches and had to beg those. Eventually, lighting a cigarette was such an effort, he didn't.

5. *Don't clog your mind with a lot of annoying trifles—forget them.*

This frees your mind for important things. Don't try to keep such trifles as shopping lists, telephone numbers, engagements in your head. Jot them down.

6. *To forget a grudge—and you should—put it on paper.*

That's Singer Dinah Shore's method. "When I'm mad," she says, "I want to say things. But that only makes it worse. So now I write instead. I have written reams of invective but no one ever sees it. I put it in my 'grudge drawer' and burn it the next day. Having got it off my chest, I forget it."

7. *Forget your work, and do a better job.*

Experts say you do your work better, finish fresher if you break it up by short rest periods. Change completely from what you are doing. If you stand ordinarily, sit or lie down. If you're seated, walk around. Forget the job. You'll return to it refreshed.

8. *Don't be a grouch—improve your disposition by forgetting gloom.*

A group of self-declared grouches in Dr. W. H. Mikesell's psychology classes at Wichita University were put on a three-months' schedule. For two months each student was to make four cheery remarks to companions each day. The third month, students were to specialize in looking on the bright side of their work. By then no further practice was needed.

9. *To forget worry, learn thought control.*

It's being done at the Thought Control Class of the Boston Dispensary. Patients who have worried themselves into a dozen kinds of diseases come here and learn the knack of substitute thinking.

10. *To forget your past failures, picture the exact opposite.*

Babe Ruth told me that in his early baseball days his frequent strike-outs plagued him with doubt every time he came to bat. To erase their memory, the Babe did this: on coming to the plate, he'd picture just one possibility—hitting it over the fence. The idea worked, with results that still top the record books.

Take a tip from Babe Ruth. Cease to remind yourself of your past failures and you'll forget them.

What Is Your *Emotional Age?*

by J. George Frederick * Condensed from GROW UP EMOTIONALLY AND HAVE FUN!

HERE's a way to measure how old you are emotionally.

If nothing has happened to warp or retard their emotional development, adults are supposed to be emotionally mature at 25 years of age. Therefore, the top mark you can get in the following quiz is 25 years old emotionally. If you come out with less than 25, you are to that extent below emotional maturity.

Answer each of the following questions by *yes* or *no.* Then refer to the answer key at the end of the questions and put down the number given for each question, according to the *yes* or *no* answer. When you finish, add up the total and divide by 25. The result is your approximate emotional age.

25 is the perfect score

22 to 24 is normal maturity

18 to 21 is just average

17 and below is adolescent

1. Am I wavering and uncertain in my aims and purposes?
2. Do my moods rise and fall constantly between elation and depression?
3. Am I either considerably sensitive (or supremely confident) · about my personal good looks?
4. Do I sometimes become very "fed up" with everybody and everything? Or want to get away from it all?
5. Am I every now and then afraid I'm an absolute failure or misfit (or every now and then convinced I'm a very wonderful person)?
6. Am I able to live away from my parents or family without greatly needing them?
7. Is my idea of the best possible enjoyment the company of the opposite sex?
8. Would I be afraid if I were left absolutely alone in the world, without parents, sisters or brothers or relatives?
9. Is it one of my keenest delights to help people and to give things to people?
10. When things go wrong, am I usually of the opinion that not myself but others are to blame?
11. Am I prone to lose my temper quickly and say things better left unsaid?
12. Am I annoyed, or hurt or ashamed when I'm in a group and nobody pays any attention to me for long stretches of time?
13. Am I prone to exaggerate, or invent tales that throw a favorable or glamorous light about me?
14. Do I like to be mysterious and aloof and insinuate vague, subtle things?

15. Am I never quite so happy as when I know I have on very "spiffy" clothes, or appearing at some "swell" place or with some very desirable companion, or when the limelight is on me?
16. Do I frequently lie or argue myself out of a tight place rather than confess I was wrong or did wrong?
17. Am I prone to let others do the "treating"— (or always insisting ostentatiously that I treat)?
18. Do I cultivate a domineering way in order to hide the truth that I'm afraid I'm too soft or easy-going?
19. Am I touchy and peculiar about sex? —afraid of it or antagonistic to it because I'm rather uncontrollably passionate; or prejudiced against it because I'm *not* very passionate or interested?
20. Am I consistently sympathetic, friendly and good chum-like to others?
21. Have I any real confidence in my ability to make my way in the world, without leaning on anyone?
22. Do I occasionally "stage a scene" or a tantrum, or a "fit" when things break very badly for me?
23. Does it frequently seem to me that people talk about me behind my back or laugh or sneer at me, or speak with double meanings, or hidden sarcasm in their words?
24. Am I tense and nervous and fretty, restless, changeful or scatter-brained?
25. Am I jealous and possessive with anyone I love, and never quite satisfied that they really love me, or that they express their adoration in the way or to the extent that I would like?

Answers to Emotional Age Test:
1. yes 8; no 19 — 2. yes 6; no 20 — 3. yes 9; no 17 — 4. yes 10; no 20 — 5. yes 4; no 29 — 6. yes 23; no 5 — 7. yes 31; no 5 — 8. yes 8; no 26 — 9. yes 36; no 2 — 10. yes 11; no 29 — 11. yes 7; no 24 — 12. yes 12; no 19 — 13. yes 6; no 21 — 14. yes 13; no 24 — 15. yes 9; no 25 — 16. yes 14; no 26 — 17. yes 9; no 19 — 18. yes 6; no 17 — 19. yes 5; no 29 — 20. yes 23; no 11 — 21. yes 36; no 10 — 22. yes 4; no 31 — 23. yes 8; no 20 — 24. yes 7; no 31 — 25. yes 12; no 22.

Pointers to Popularity

1. Always say less than you think. Cultivate a low, persuasive voice.
2. Keep promises, no matter what cost.
3. Be interested in others. Let them, however humble, feel that you regard them as important.
4. Be cheerful. Hide your worries under a smile.
5. Keep an open mind. Discuss, but don't argue.
6. Be careful of another's feelings. Wit and humor at the other fellow's expense are rarely worth the effort.
7. Pay no attention to ill-natured remarks about you. Simply live so that nobody will believe them.
8. Don't overstress your rights. Do your work, be patient, and you will be rewarded.

—*Pere Marquette Magazine*

The Impression You Make Depends Upon the Colors You Wear!

by W. Beran Wolfe, M. D.

Condensed from THE WOMAN

WHAT woman has not asked herself the question, "Which colors are best for me?" Every woman is enough of a practical psychologist to know that she looks better in some colors than in others, though more often than not her psychology is purely and simply intuitive.

Are there any good psychological rules for pink and purple, for brown and blue and the rest of them?

Red is the most stimulating color in the spectrum. It translates its vivacious psychology not only to the wearer but to the beholder. Especially in depressing times red is wholesome and stimulating. It is a good psychological rule to wear red when you feel "blue." Because of red's tonic effect every woman should have a red dress and a red hat.

That is, every woman but the woman who simply cannot wear red because of its conflict with her skin tones, and the nervous, highstrung woman. Large women, unless they are striking beauties, must watch

their reds, and will do better to choose the burgundy or claret side of red rather than crimson or tile reds. But with these exceptions, every woman should have a red dress.

Green is predominantly the color of youth, of peace, of freedom from stress and disturbances. A deep rich grass green costume always brings with it a breath of the out-of-doors, and in the severe confines of an office it offers an especially pleasing contrast. Green is a good color to wear in any home or office where jarring personalities create nervous tension.

But beware of olive green. Only a woman whose own colorings are extremely high, the auburn-haired beauty or the henna-haired woman whose hair is natural, can dare to wear olive green.

Psychologically speaking, yellow is the color which most appeals to children. The young woman, therefore, who wishes to accentuate her own youthfulness will do well to let this color predominate in her attire. Any woman who has to do with young children will find this sunny color of great value in attracting the attention of her small charges.

There are a great many people who, because of their emotional immaturity and really childish attitude toward the world, prefer this color to all others. Following her natural preferences is not a good move for such a young woman if she is in a position where she must make a grownup impression. Let her wear yellow on her holidays, on her playdays, but not in her office.

Black, especially if it is in a material like satin which gives it enlivening highlights, tends to make the young woman more dignified. If you are in a position where you have to create "front," where you have to be the first contact with important strangers, black, well relieved by white at the neck and at the cuffs, with a spot of color here and there to give a youthful air, can always be relied upon.

When you are in doubt as to what color to choose for any occasion wear black set off with a dash of white, or white and red. More women look well in a smart black dress than in any other color. The exception to this rule is the slender, dark woman whose skin is sallow. Black will give her a funeral look. Large women look better in black than in any other color because black most easily melts into every background. Blond women with good color wear black best of all, especially if they set it off with a

dash of color in gems or accessories.

Brown gives an air of fresh out-of-door sportiness to the young woman. Older women should guard against this color, but the young woman who has not yet seen twenty-five can wear it with impunity. Any color—and you can put this down as a psychological rule—worn in solid shades, and unrelieved by the addition of complementary colors, is likely to make a monotonous and drab effect. Brown, therefore, one of the worst offenders when it is dull, should never be worn solid. Spots of yellow or of orange or of vermilion make brown interesting, and raise its psychological "tone."

Blues which are unrelieved or dull in tone are almost as depressing as brown and are as much in need of being "picked up" by white or bright accessories. The young woman who likes brown or navy blue because they are sensible and conservative and smart should be careful in choosing her weaves, so that the actual weave of the fabrics she wears, helps to relieve the monotony of the color itself. Young women who wish to appear more mature may attempt fuchsia and burgundy and bougainvillea purples, but with all such colors there

❀ ❀ ❀ ❀ ❀ ❀ ❀ ❀ ❀ ❀ ❀

If you are ever in doubt as to what color to wear for any occasion, play safe. Wear a simple black dress, set off with a dash of white at the neck or the cuffs.

is the danger that maturity may be overstepped.

The pastel shades are the pre-eminent domain of the young woman. Beige for business, light blues for evening for the blondes, while the brunettes may avail themselves of more daring shades in order to bring out their natural colors.

In connection with the wise use of color there are two optical principles which it is interesting and valuable to know. Ninety-nine out of a hundred women do not understand these principles because they are derived from an abstruse and theoretical polka dot.

Have you ever looked into the starry heavens? Have you ever looked at a meadow full of daisies or wildflowers? If you have, you have no doubt felt a tremendous sense of "lift." For some reason which no psychiatrist has ever been able to explain fully, bright dots on a dark field have an ecstatic effect on the human soul.

Apply this principle to your clothes. Put on a polka-dot scarf when you call on a sick friend. Wear a polka-dot dress when you have to call on a gruff old executive. Haven't you noticed that women who wear polka-dot effects usually are happy women?

The second optico-psychological principle is just as deeply rooted in mysterious human reactions. Have you ever driven your automobile through the country at night and had your headlights pick up an unseen cat's eyes somewhere at the side of the road? Haven't you been fascinated by those two shining spots of color and light? Haven't you been compelled to look at a beautiful woman at a ball whose eyes shone brilliantly?

The principle is used often by psychiatrists in hypnosis. *Two bright spots on a dark background are the most compelling attention-getters in the world!*

But how many women who want to make an impression on a man, how many who want to *fix* one man's attention on them know enough psychology to put two bright spots of white or yellow close together somewhere on a dark dress, or two jeweled clips for the same effect somewhere on a hat or near the neck line? Try it the next time you want to hold the center of a man's gaze.

≫≫-≫≫-≫≫-≫≫-≫≫ �֎ ≪≪-≪≪-≪≪-≪≪-≪≪

A NATION-WIDE Personality Test given by 80 psychologists showed that *social dancing* is the best of all social games for improving personality. It teaches you how to meet people, how to behave in a graceful, socially acceptable manner, improves your conversational ability, develops self-confidence and does it in a most delightful and inspiring way.

—*Albert Edward Wiggam, D. Sc.*

How to Act on a DATE

by Katherine Hartley Frings   *   *   *   Condensed from MOVIE MIRROR

THERE is one awkward moment which every young man dreads when he goes to call for his date. That is the one which he is usually forced to pass with the girl's mother or father, or both, while he waits for his date to appear. It's up to the girl to eliminate this embarrassment by being ready when he arrives and by personally greeting him at the door. Then it is proper for her to ask him in, so that he may say good evening to one or both of the parents, but this need take only a few minutes. It is up to the girl to do everything possible in her own home to make him feel at ease. If he is an extremely shy young man, she may even wait to thank him for the flowers he sent until they get into the car, because most young men do not like to be thanked for something in front of others.

A smart young girl will also make sure that her handbag has ample space for the cosmetics, etc., which she wishes to take with her, so that she need not ask the young man to carry anything for her. Boys hate to have their pockets full of female paraphernalia.

One of the most perplexing problems is what to do about each other's arms while walking. The answer is that nothing should be done. The young man may possibly place his hand at the girl's elbow, but the girl should never grab his arm, which makes walking difficult and also makes him feel silly. The girl should walk just a little in advance of him, and both will look better if their arms are free.

A decided "don't"—when the head waiter starts leading you to your table, don't hang back, sneaking a look into your compact. It's not only bad taste to take out your compact at this time, but this delay on your part may force the young man to walk in advance of you, and this is entirely wrong. The girl follows the head waiter first, and the young man follows her. It is not good taste to stand and argue about whether or not he is taking you to a good table.

Follow the captain to the table he indicates. Then, if you prefer another one, say so to your escort and allow him to ask for a better one.

Faux pas about ordering are almost always made by the girl, and so these "do's" and "don'ts" are mostly for her. In the first place, the young man will ask you what you want to eat, and you should tell him, not the waiter. In fact, you should have no conversation at all with the waiter (and never, never kid with him!). Your escort, after you tell him what you want, will pass on your order to the waiter and then follow it with his order.

In the same way, as the dinner progresses, you should never hail the waiter. If you want something extra, or if he has forgotten something, then again state your wants to your escort and let him take care of calling the waiter and asking him for service.

When you get ready to dance, it is usually wise for you to remove your corsage from your left shoulder, so that the pin will not annoy your partner—and also to save the flowers from being crushed. You may put them on your right shoulder, or you may just leave them at the table.

If you have trouble keeping your flowers pinned on, don't ask the boy to help you with the pinning; he'll feel all fingers at such a delicate task. There's usually an attendant in the ladies' salon who will be glad to help you.

Another important "don't" for girls—don't flirt or show unusual attention to the orchestra leader. Your escort resents such a division of your attention, and he has a right to. In the same way, he doesn't enjoy hav-ing you sing in his ears; he also resents having you talk to some other couple over his shoulder.

If you're smart, you'll be very careful not to mar his suit with powder or lipstick marks; but he will like to sense just the faintest aroma of perfume on your hair.

Girls often wonder, too, if it is proper for them to applaud after a dance. It's best to leave this invitation for an encore to your partner. When the music stops, remember not to hang on to his arm. Just stand by him quietly; don't wiggle around awkwardly. While dancing, it is best to leave your handbag at the table. Never put it under your chair. When it's time for the check, you should refrain from trying to see how much it is. If you want to repair your make-up in the ladies' room before leaving, this is a good time to do so while your escort is taking care of the check and tip. Incidentally, consider the young man's pocketbook. You will make a hit if you order the less expensive regular dinner instead of ordering à la carte.

All youthful awkwardness really comes from a lack of knowledge. With the above points in mind, even a first date ought to go quite smoothly. Here, in conclusion, are a few points to aid in popularity.

In case a girl wonders how she can return a boy's entertainment, she can always invite him anywhere, to the theater or to a dance, or even to dinner, provided payment for the evening's entertainment is arranged for in advance. If a young man has taken you out a number of times, this is quite proper and very thoughtful. But never give him the money to pay the bill. Never suggest a Dutch treat, either, after you have once accepted his invitation.

In a car a girl should remember not to sit too close to her escort with her arm linked through his, as this really endangers his driving. Another point for all girls to remember: If you should use the car mirror to look at

yourself, be sure to put it back at its usual angle for driving convenience. Nothing annoys a man more than to find his wind-shield mirror twisted around.

Lastly, a young girl may give her picture to a boy if she knows him quite well and if he expresses a desire for it, but it is not considered good taste to sign it, even with just her first name. An elaborate statement of affection on a photograph may seem ridiculous and be embarrassing later.

* * * * * ★ * * * * *

Do You Have A Sense of Humor?

Here are the scores for the test on pages 71 and 72. Draw circles around the numbers that correspond to the items you checked—one in each of the eight columns. If, for instance, you checked item "d" under Question I, you would circle the number on line "d" under column I—number 2, in this case.

Item	QUESTIONS							
	I	II	III	IV	V	VI	VII	VIII
a.	3	5	4	2	1	5	4	1
b.	4	2	3	3	2	3	1	5
c.	1	1	1	5	4	4	3	2
d.	2	3	2	4	5	1	5	4
e.	5	4	5	1	3	2	2	3

To get the score for your sense of humor add the numbers you circled for all of the questions. If the sum is below 20, your sense of humor can be improved; between 20 and 30 you are average; between 31 and 40 your sense of humor is way above par—or you've been generous with yourself.

𝓗𝓮 𝓕𝓸𝓾𝓷𝓭 𝓪 𝓜𝓪𝓰𝓲𝓬

FOOTPATH to POPULARITY

by Jerome Beatty

Reprinted from the AMERICAN MAGAZINE

UNTIL I went to see Arthur Murray, I hadn't met a teacher of ballroom dancing for nineteen years, and I was utterly ignorant of the new developments in the business world. I thought dancing was moving the feet in time to music. I learned that dancing is the new way to popularity, a simple method of selling yourself, your apples, or your machine for wrapping roller skates in cellophane.

Business men are going into it in a big way. Youngsters just out of college are discovering that if you want to work for Mr. Uriah Q. Minklemotter in his ice cream factory, the best way is to dance well with his wife and daughters.

Arthur Murray perhaps has done more than any other one person to help men sell with their feet everything from advertising to zebras. He has taught the walk, the chassé, the waltz, the balance, and the pivot by mail, over the radio, in moving pictures, in newspapers, in magazines, and in his resident school, which now occupies all of his time.

In his schools he employs as many as 1500 dancing teachers. He has turned the teaching of dancing into big business; the gross annual income is nearly $5,000,000. His New York studios, in which 200 teachers may give private lessons at one time, fill 12 office-building floors, and in the busy season sixteen girls are needed to handle the appointments, which begin at 10 o'clock in the morning.

Most of his pupils are men—a majority of them business men. For the very timid, Murray has a back elevator which takes them straight to a studio, and they steal in and out unseen, as though they were robbing a chicken coop. The Prince of Wales, in 1924, used this elevator. So did the prime minister of a British colony.

On the wall of Murray's office is an autographed photograph of one of New York's richest and most prominent society girls, in the gown in which she was presented at Court, in London. Murray, as a rule, gives no personal lessons, but this girl's mother insisted that he must teach her daughter.

"The fee will be $5,000," said Murray.

"That is perfectly satisfactory," said the mother.

For that price he gave the daughter 100 hours of instruction and turned her into a very good dancer, indeed. If worst comes to worst she should be able to sell many carloads of cast-iron fire dogs.

Murray's pupils range from the average middle-class family to the Park Avenue rich and ex-rich. His teachers are, mostly, college men and women. A few are ambitious girls from Social Register families whose fortunes have tumbled. Eighty per cent of the teachers are girls—not entirely because of the fact that most of Murray's pupils are men. Women learn more quickly from women than from men, because they learn to imitate their teacher.

Arthur Murray became a dancing teacher against his will and in spite of vigorous parental objection. As a youth he suffered the pangs of a wallflower for two whole years. Eventually he became an excellent dancer and found that teaching was a simple way to make a living, but time and again he tried to break away. He attempted to become an architect, an advertising man, a hotel manager, a photographer, a newspaper reporter, and a printing salesman.

But finally, when a sophomore at Georgia School of Technology, in Atlanta, where he was taking a course in business administration, he added up his receipts from dancing lessons and found that in the preceding twelve months he had made $15,000.

A thousand boys and girls were attending his children's classes. The names of hundreds of Atlanta's socially elect were in his appointment books. That wasn't enough. He left college and set about extending his field.

He had studied mail-order merchandising in the business course and immediately set about to try it on dancing. He made diagrams, had movies shot and illustrations drawn. He wrote advertisements and circulars and lessons, and made a nuisance of himself trying them out on every guest at the hotel who would listen.

Murray arranged to sell his correspondence course from a New York address while he remained in Atlanta. At first it was a terrific flop. Murray was $10,000 in the red before he discovered his mistakes. His first error was in giving his pupils detailed pictures of people doing the steps. The point of view, he discovered, was all wrong.

"People learn to dance," he told me, "by looking down at their own feet, not by looking across the ballroom at somebody else's. When I gave them a bird's-eye view of the steps, and simplified them, the pupils were able to learn."

His lessons revised, he started to

find out what was the matter with his advertising. It had been rather aimless, usually telling about what a fine dancer Arthur Murray was. He began to analyze his own case. He asked himself, "Why did I take up dancing when I was a kid?"

Being a frank sort of person, he admitted that it was to make friends, to become popular, and he realized that dancing had cured his boyish bashfulness and his appalling fear of girls.

He realized now that his early failures as a salesman had occurred because he was timid, afraid to state his case boldly, and that the cause of this timidity was the fact that he knew he wasn't properly equipped.

On the dance floor he had been a different person. Through practice, he had made himself the best dancer of all the young men in the neighborhood. Girls were glad to dance with him. Boys looked up to him.

The correspondence school grew until it occupied an entire floor of an office building. After a year or so, men and women began to drop in to ask Murray if he wouldn't give them private lessons. At first he said, "No!"

Then he curtained off a little room at one end of the offices, installed a phonograph and a teacher. Soon there were three teachers. The private studios began to crowd back the mailing department. And now, directing 1500 instructors, he has abandoned the correspondence courses and he's a dancing master, in spite of himself, again.

But he thinks of himself still as a business man. Now, as always, he would attack with murderous intent any person who called him "Professor." However, if you insist, he will give you 100 hours of personal instruction for $5,000. Is that being a business man? I'll say.

>>> >>> >>> >>> <<< <<< <<< <<<

YOUR NOSE

If You Have . . .	*You . . .*
A nose well built up at the bridge	Have creative, constructive imagination and constructive ability; can put yourself in the other fellow's place; like to create and uplift; take pride in work, family, and race
A protruding nose, built out at the end or coming to a sharp point	Have destructive imagination and ability; curiosity; like to take things apart to see what makes them go; like to ask questions and investigate
A nose that is built up both at the bridge and at the end	Are artistic; like to find out about things, then create
A nose that tilts up at the end	Are argumentative, critical, inquisitive, even saucy; but alert
A small nose, ending close to the face	Like to mind your own business; resent meddling; may be self-centered
Broad nostrils	Love melody, and are emotionally stirred by it

—NANCY VAN COURT in *The American Magazine*

For Dancers

Don't look resolved to do or die.

● Don't look resolved to do or die. That's dancing the hard way—hard on your partner.

● Don't grasp the girl around the waist—hiking her dress two inches shorter than the designer intended.

● Don't leave your mark on a man's lapel. When removing powder and lipstick stains he may also remove your name from his list.

● Don't be a "solo dancer."

● Don't apologize for your poor dancing. She'll still wish she had stayed at home with a good book.

Don't hike the girl's dress up the back.

● Don't shift your right hand up and down her spine like a chiropractor — or an indecisive saxophone player.

● Don't dance just once with your wife, and park her for the rest of the evening.

● Don't dance for the onlooker's benefit. It is more considerate to please your partner.

Pull in that hip Before you trip.

● Don't be a "floor hog."

Arthur Murray *teachers suggest you heed these* WARNINGS:

*If solo's your rage,
Go hire a stage.*

● Don't wear large buttons or ornaments in front. You'll make an impression—but not the right kind.

● Don't chatter incessantly while dancing—you may drown out the music.

● Don't eye all the other men while dancing. Flirts are a pain in the masculine pride.

● Don't forget that being backed around the room is not a girl's idea of fun.

● If you can't talk and dance at the same time —try dancing.

● Don't try intricate steps that your partner can't follow. She may be impressed by your dancing—but she may wind up the evening with a desire to say, "Don't think it hasn't been fun—because it *hasn't!*"

*Her letter S
Denotes distress.*

*Don't rest your head
and grind face-powder
into his dinner jacket.*

● Don't give helpful pointers while dancing. It makes you sound fault-finding.

● Don't steer your partner around the floor like a bicycle.

● Don't chew gum in time to music. Don't chew gum in your partner's ear. Maybe . . . don't chew gum!

● Don't dance side-saddle.

...DON'T'S *for Dancers*

Don't be a floor hog.

From "brutal benders"
Give us defenders.

- Don't be so serious. Leave your business face at the office when you step out.

- Don't say you *hate* dancing just because you don't know how.

- If you want to lead a man to the altar—don't lead him on the dance floor.

- Don't let old-fashioned dancing date you!

- When you make a misstep, don't blame the orchestra.

The cheek-to-cheek
No longer chic.

- Don't brag "I never had a lesson in my life."

- Don't keep on dancing for "politeness' sake" when neither of you is having fun.

- Don't pump your arms or flounce your elbows to help you keep time.

- Don't pull the girl forward so that her derrière waves in the breeze.

- Don't dance passively—be glad you're alive.

Dragging a dame,
A weary game.

On Walking Correctly

THOUGH men and girls face different ways on the dance floor they must both learn to walk correctly. Since the Man's instructions are simpler I give them first.

MAN'S INSTRUCTIONS:

The Man walks *forward* most of the time in dancing. Consequently he always starts off with his *left* foot first.

GIRL'S INSTRUCTIONS:

The Girl walks *backward* (as the Man steps forward) always with her right foot first. Thus the two partners are in step together.

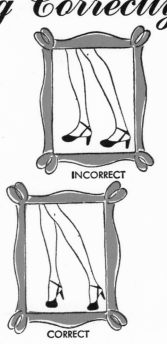

INCORRECT

CORRECT

WHEN YOU DANCE:
(POINTS FOR BOTH TO REMEMBER)

Lift the feet slightly off the floor when walking—never let them drag or scrape the floor. The heels should *never* touch the floor when dancing backward; when walking forward the heels may touch the floor, but only *after* the toes.

After you have become proficient you may dance any way you choose, but while learning dance only on your toes or the ball of the foot.

Always move naturally, easily, comfortably; without strain or self-consciousness *and* without exaggerating the steps.

To give spring to your steps, practice rising up and down on your toes, taking long slow walking steps around the room in the Line of Direction.

She travels 3000 miles a year—on her own two feet. But it's wonderful work, if you can get it

Arthur Murray Girl

by Marjorie Mueller Freer   *   *   *   Condensed from SHE MAGAZINE

WHEN did the Arthur Murray girl first appear on the dancing horizon? Back in 1923 when, at the insistence of his public, Mr. Murray gave up his correspondence course in dancing with its by now classic "How I became Popular Overnight" advertising slogan and opened a studio of personalized instruction in New York. Eleven East 43rd Street with its one hundred and fifty private studios is still the Murray headquarters. But now there are also branch studios in fifty-six cities and sixty-seven seasonal resorts throughout the country. Before the war, Murray teachers were also a regular feature of every first-class steamship cruise, and will presumably be so again.

The average age of the Arthur Murray girl is between twenty-one and twenty-eight and the national roll call approximates thirteen hundred. War time demand for her is such that the original five to six month training period has been pared down to less than three months. But no corners are cut. The work is simply more in-tensive and is personally directed by Mr. Murray who believes that training must never stop—which is why there are continuous refresher courses for the faculty. Even teachers who have been with the organization many years are required to attend these Post Graduate Dance Sessions. Receptionists are instructed to make no appointments during these classes which feature new steps and changes in teaching methods. As a result Murray instructors are always abreast or even a little ahead of the dancing times.

This brings us down to your own chances of becoming an Arthur Murray girl. They are good. But there are any number of hurdles. And these keep the profession on a high and select level. How many steps you initially know is of little account. Grace and an inborn sense of rhythm are your most important terpsichorean assets. However, that's only part of the story. No ivy clad, tradition-bound finishing school admits students with more care than does Arthur

Murray his future dancing teachers.

The first step is up to you. If you live in or near New York City, you watch for Murray ads in the metropolitan dailies (particularly the *Times* and *Tribune*) which state that teacher-training classes will shortly begin.

Step number two is to present yourself for a preliminary interview. A personable appearance is necessary, but you don't have to be a pin-up girl to qualify. As a matter of fact, young and delightful Mrs. Murray who manages all the branch studios (and is mother of the Murray twins) assured me that too glamourous a facade stands in the way of a dancing teaching career. This springs from the belief that a girl with really spectacular looks seldom takes more than a superficial interest in anyone but herself.

Step number three is the Bernreuter Personality test which you take if you've given an intelligent and pleasing impression. This quiz, by the way, establishes whether or not you are an introvert or extrovert, but is chiefly instrumental in singling out neurotics. If you're an extrovert, you have every chance of becoming an excellent teacher. But introverts who can come out of their shells do well too because they have a fellow-feeling for the shy pupil and know from their own experience how best to make him feel at ease.

Your personality test over, you are ushered past acres of executive offices into The Presence. In his red-panelled headquarters, Arthur Murray makes you feel very much at home. You chat pleasantly of this and that—particularly of your dancing ambitions, but this is really an examination of another kind. How are you at making conversation? How serious are you about a future as an Arthur Murray dancing instructor? Are you going to give it everything you've got, or is it just a phase in a succession of career samplings? (Marriage is the only logical reason for leaving.) Once you've made the point that you are serious about dance-teaching as a career the maestro samples your dancing (yes, he dances with you himself so take along smelling salts in case you're overcome with the glory of it all!).

Yes, you've made it! The Head gives his nod of approval which means you have natural dancing ability in addition to a pleasing personality and intelligence. You are now an Arthur Murray trainee. But the preliminary hurdles are nothing to what's ahead of you now. The next few weeks you're going through the most intensive type of training conceivable. You won't be paid while training, but if you're sailing close to the wind financially, arrangements can be made to draw against your future salary. You learn how to dance as though you'd never before heard the meaning of the words. Your dancing is completely remade.

Make-up and dress are not taken up formally. You learn rather by example. Different members of the Murray staff told me that even after a few weeks this imitative method produces subtle and important changes in a girl's appearance. Your make-up is judiciously flattering, clothes and even costume colors now enhance and high-light you as a person for your own future students to emulate.

But suppose we see what actually goes on in the preparatory period. Throughout the training your hours are the same—10 A.M. to 6 P.M. There are numerous sitting-down sessions devoted to text-book work, names of steps, sequence of steps and lectures on teaching technique. Incidentally you also quickly learn to discard your flattering, high-heeled opera pumps and to wear comfortable, medium-heeled sandals.

The first week is the hard one. Your dancing seems so *gauche* beside the finished technique of the full-fledged instructors. Then there is the difficulty of learning the man's as well as the girl's part of all the steps. Worst of all is the shyness that assails you when Mr. Murray, school supervisors, and high-ranking teachers observe and try out your dancing. Your dance ego was never lower.

Surprisingly, the second week is fun. By now you're invited to attend the regular teachers' meetings which are conducted by Mr. Murray. You see many familiar faces among the teachers, have a nodding and speaking acquaintance with a large number of them, and have begun to make friends. You also feel closer to teaching because various pupils have visited your class, exhibited their dancing for you with their own teachers, and have chatted informally with you and your

If you have any personal dance problems, please do not hesitate to write, telephone or visit your nearest Arthur Murray Studio for aid. Our teachers will be glad to demonstrate any of the steps taught in this book.

fellow classmates. And when you hear these pupils say how much dancing lessons have meant to them, you're more anxious than ever to begin the real work of teaching. Now, instead of dreading Mr. Murray's visits, you look forward to them, and watch his style of dancing with an appreciative and hawk-like eye as he demonstrates with one of the other girls or the teacher. You know just enough dancing to have a burning desire for more. You feel perfectly at home in the studio . . . even to calling the elevator man "Pop."

The third week you're champing at the bit and really raring to show what you can do. This is also a period of examinations—four written ones and a personal dancing-teaching test by Mr. Murray. Your self-confidence has increased because you've followed his advice and taught everything you learned to those of your friends and family who are willing to play guinea pigs.

According to Mrs. Murray, there isn't one new teacher who doesn't have stage fright when she is face to face with her first pupil. "My mind went blank," and, "I was petrified," are some of the typical remarks. "But," added "Madame Big Boss" as she is affectionately termed by the staff, "it can't really be true because new teachers are so earnest and conscientious that pupils are always pleased."

So six weeks after your admission, you are a full-fledged instructor teaching from four to six hours a day and earning an initial salary of $40 a week. You're adept at the Fox Trot, Waltz, Rumba, Samba and Jitterbug. You also know Group dances suitable for children's classes, parties and canteens. There's a call for part-time teachers too, so if you can only give a certain number of hours in the evening, you can earn up to $30 a week. Since you're very much taken with your work, you'll only leave the organization (if then!) when you marry.

As an Arthur Murray girl, you are also in line for promotions. Much, of course, depends upon your natural ability. Common sense and a generous slice of humor help in getting on with students, fellow teachers and superiors. A successful instructor can either become a supervisor in charge of a floor with ten or twelve teachers under her (salaries in this bracket start at $60 a week), or manage a resort branch in a first-class hotel following it up with a similar winter job. This means you would run the social dances of the hotel as well as do regu-

lar teaching. The main branch studios are managed by those who also began as Arthur Murray instructors. Several branch managers are earning over $25,000 a year.

A typical teaching day at the Arthur Murray studio might include pupils ranging from a prominent psychiatrist to a nineteen-year-old sailor. You might be sent to teach a class at a hospital for overseas wounded or to a private house like that of Mr. John D. Rockefeller, Jr.

Teaching at a branch studio does not differ from teaching at the main studio. Here too the work is highly engrossing and satisfying. To quote an attractive young teacher at one of the out-of-town studios:

"As far as I'm concerned, I like to teach because I like people, and of course, because I love to dance. One of the things I enjoy most about dancing is meeting so many people, and it's interesting to discover how similar they really are. If they act haughty or cocky, it's just because they're painfully self-conscious. As soon as they realize that everyone makes just about the same mistakes they relax and really start to have a good time."

Like every happy, normal American girl, the Arthur Murray girl looks forward to marriage, and, in most cases, she marries. If anything, the Murray dancing teacher's matrimonial opportunities are enhanced because her training has made her tactful, added to her poise and self-confidence; lessons in good posture have improved her looks, and association with other teachers has added style sense—all plusses on the side of personal attractiveness.

Added to her many other advantages, the Arthur Murray girl travels —three thousand miles a year—but she does it all on her own two feet, waltzing, rumba-ing, jitterbugging, foxtrotting and samba-ing around the studio floor to the tune of ten miles a day! Yes, join the Arthur Murray girls and your heart as well as your feet will be light, and you'll not only see the dancing world—you'll be a joyous, dynamic part of it!

The Good Hostess

HERE ARE FIFTEEN QUESTIONS on whether you are a good hostess. They should be answered with either a "yes" or a "no." When you have faced all the questions sincerely, add up your number of affirmative answers and see by how many they outnumber the negative, or vice versa. The good hostess should have eleven or more "yes"-es. If you score less than eight, keep this test by you and study it very carefully, especially when you have visitors coming. It should help you to happier friendships.

1. Do you study compatibility when selecting your guests?
2. If you have one visitor more important than the others do you show equal consideration and courtesy to all?
3. When entertaining do you see that practically all preparations are completed *before* the guests arrive?
4. Do you aim at being natural rather than competitive in the hospitality you provide?
5. Are you an easy conversationalist?
6. Can you make people soon feel at home?
7. Do you make a point of showing interest in other people's pet subjects?
8. Have you a friendly smile and manner?
9. Do you remember and prepare for your friends' dietetic idiosyncrasies?
10. Are you continually and *unobtrusively* attentive to the wants of your guests?
11. Can you quickly put nervous people at ease and draw them into things?
12. Do you avoid offering only trouble-saving "pot-luck" to your intimate friends?
13. When you entertain, do you aim wholly at giving people a good time, avoiding any attempt at ostentation?
14. Are you prepared to take real care and trouble to entertain your guests?
15. Are your invitations accepted with alacrity?—*The Psychologist, England.*

A newspaperman once received $1000 for three words. In these sizzlegrams he has adapted his principles of successful selling to help you personally

How to Sell Yourself—WITH WORDS

BY ELMER WHEELER ✺ Condensed from WORD MAGIC

ABOUT ten years ago a newspaper man, Elmer Wheeler, developed an idea for increasing sales through a more effective use of words. He became one of the best paid writers in America. He often has received as much as $1000 for a three-word phrase. He has now adapted his principles of successfull selling to help you meet those many personal situations confronting you at home, in the office and in society. See how many of these sizzlegrams you can solve.

Sizzlegram A

What Words Make the Best Impression When You're Being Introduced?

1. "I'm very glad to meet you."
2. "This is a real pleasure."
3. "How do you do?"
4. "How are you?"
5. "I've often heard of you."
6. "Bill often mentions you, Mr. Green."
7. "Hello."

Sizzlegram B

If Your Hubby Always Likes You in One Color Only, How Can You "Sell" Him on Other Colors?

1. "I'm going to wear blue today."
2. "Why can't I wear other colors?"

3. "People think you buy me *only one red* dress a year."
4. "Look at the way Mrs. Brown wears blue."
5. "I'll wear blue for a change, just to make the red dresses look prettier when I wear them."
6. "I get so sick of red dresses."
7. "What other colors look well on me, darling?"

Sizzlegram C

Do You Have a Friend Who Is Suffering from an Inferiority Complex? There Is a Sizzlegram That Will Help Him.

1. "You're as smart as anyone else you know."
2. "I suppose you think you're not going to be president some day."

3. "Have you noticed how stupid Fredric White is about mechanics?"
4. "Why don't you snap out of it?"
5. "It's all because you took the wrong course at school."
6. "Why don't you see a doctor?"
7. "Why don't you stop thinking about your weak points?"

Sizzlegram D

How Can You Get Your Husband to Have Better Table Manners?

1. "If Emily Post could only see you!"
2. "In what boarding house did you learn to eat?"
3. "You certainly never saw the *inside* of a finishing school with those manners."
4. "And to think I married you!"
5. "You're so neat *otherwise!*"
6. "I like the way Mr. Brown handles his knife and fork."
7. "Such table manners!"

Tested Answers

Sizzlegram A

"I've often heard of you."

"Bill often mentions you, Mr. Green."

"This is a *real* pleasure."

These three answers are psychologically correct; they are different, yet not too much so to make you eccentric.

"I've often heard of you" is a real compliment to people if the remark is honest.

"Bill often mentions you, Mr. Green" compliments the one to whom you are being introduced and also Bill.

"This is a real pleasure" if spoken sincerely, will win a friend quickly for you when you cannot honestly use either of the other two salutations.

"Pleased to meet you," "How are you?" and other trite expressions leave no impression on people, and you might just as well grunt and nod.

Win people in ten seconds with your first ten words upon being introduced. Your first ten words will influence their opinion of you for many an hour to come. Above all, don't make fun of people's names, or mispronounce them. A person's name is important to *him*, even if it is "Abernathy," "Plushbottom," or "Ebenezer."

Sizzlegram B

"People think you buy me *only one red dress* a year."

"I'll wear blue for a change, just to make the red dresses look prettier when I wear them."

Either of these may work on hubby. The first sentence reflects on hubby's spending qualities, not on you. It may hurt his pride and cause him to rear up and get you a blue-and-brown dress, "*just to show those gossips I'm no tightwad.*"

The second sentence is equally tactful, and flatters *him* somewhat. He'll agree that by wearing other colors the red ones of his choice will look twice as pretty. Never come right out and tell him he's all wet, for he fell in love with you, no doubt, in that one color and can see no others. Wean him into other colors rather than make a sudden jump from red to blue.

Sizzlegram C

"Have you noticed how stupid Fredric White is about mechanics?"

This is the best thing to say. Dr. Donald Laird, of Colgate University's Department of Psychology, advises in a magazine article that an excellent antidote for feelings of inferiority "is to look at the weak points of others for a change, and—above all else—to spend more time in thinking about our own strong points."

Help your friend to see the weak points in his friends and add a few words of sincere praise for him. Don't use a member of your own set as the stupid example, and choose a subject on which your friend is good. You'll find lots of inferiority complexes around these days. Why not "go to work" on one of them for your own satisfaction? Don't be insistent about it, or your subject will want to know, "What the devil's the matter with you?"

Sizzlegram D

"You're so neat *otherwise!*"

This will flatter him into being neater. It compliments him in a way that makes him want to be as careful about his table manners as about other things.

Most men live 70 miles an hour at their work and fail to slow up when food is before them. They need just a kind reminder now and then. Sarcasm will give him indigestion—and you an attack of migraine! Holding up the neighbor's husband for a model, as we've long ago found out, never works on your man. Shaming him, tactfully, is better than shoving him obviously. Subtlety and consideration always pay dividends.

~~~~~~~~~~◎~~~~~~~~~~

How Are Your Manners?

ETIQUETTE is just another name for good manners, and good manners are as definite an asset as cash. They help one to make friends, they make one welcome at a party, they are aids to getting jobs, they give poise and assurance, and they provide an armor against the pricks of a critical world. A knowledge of manners, or the lack of it, is usually as conspicuous as though the armor were made of shining metal, and there is no imitation.

ONE of the commonest inconsistencies prevalent in the teens is the habit of talking contemptuously about etiquette in spite of feeling a secret awe of it. Actually no one who is quite bright scorns a knowledge of etiquette. It is probable that not even unrequited love has caused so much anguish as not knowing how to behave in a conspicuous moment. The bitter pill of losing your once-true love can be swallowed in private, but not the artichoke served at a dinner party.—MARJORIE HILLIS in *Good Housekeeping.*

Do you get along with people?

by Eleanor Hunter

BAD DISPOSITIONS may seem like minor evils. We *can* stand them, and so we do. But that's not saying *how* we do it—at what cost, at what inestimable damage.

Let me give you a few instances that have come to my attention recently.

Frank Hubbell had been having a pretty hard time with his business, and hadn't been able to take much money home. His wife had let her maid go and had been getting crosser and crosser with the extra house work. Of course it was hard on her, but her nastiness didn't help any. Especially this particular night when Frank needed a little building up and she lit into him with remarks about his being a failure who couldn't provide for his family as other men did. It was just too much. Frank went out and got drunk—good and drunk. The next morning, as luck would have it, a really big opportunity stuck its nose inside his door—and quickly withdrew. They couldn't take a chance on a man so obviously the worse for a spree.

Mary Jones worked desperately hard on her lessons—perhaps to build up a defense against the unpleasantness at home, the constant bickering between her parents. Now, they had turned on her. She had been scolded for her slowness at doing the dishes, the untidiness of her room, the fact that she was unsociable. She'd better hurry up and get a job, they said, for she'd never get a husband. That morning Mary had a physics examination and, try as she would, she just couldn't think. She was in such a fog of discouragement, she couldn't summon the energy necessary to tackle that exam with vigor. She failed it.

Ted Daniels had a vile disposition. He really wielded the whip in his family. He snarled and growled and everyone jumped to do his bidding. Now he was walking the streets alone. His wife had got a divorce and the children had gone with her. The blow had been pretty bad. He loved his children. I think he even loved his wife. He knew he was at fault but he didn't know how to help it. He had never before realized that love and companionship are two things that he couldn't command with any kind of whip.

You think these are extreme cases? That's only because I've picked the dramatic moments. In every one of them, there had been months of un-dramatic but nonetheless painful, dis-agreeable evenings culminating in the disasters I have described.

There isn't much you can do about the other fellow's temperament, but there is a lot each one of us can do about his own. And it's highly pos-sible that we may need to, even though we don't realize it.

I got one of the biggest surprises of my life one time when I was scold-ing my son. As I started in with my criticisms suddenly something in his face stopped me dead. It was a kind of horror—fascinated horror, like that of a bird confronted with a snake. As if he would like to get away from me but couldn't. As if he'd like to fight back but couldn't. I stopped. "I'm sorry, son," I murmured, "I guess you're taking this harder than I meant it."

And that was a fact. I hadn't meant it as viciously as it sounded to him. I never had thought that I was mean or had a bad disposition, but it was evident my son did think so. "Maybe that's the way it always is with people who let go and say harsh, cruel things," I thought to myself. "Maybe they don't mean them the way they sound. They don't even realize they have bad dispositions."

Perhaps they don't know what they are doing to others. They don't know they may be hurting them more cruelly than if they actually struck them; they may be killing their self-esteem and self-confidence. They don't realize how they are un-dermining their strength and ability, poisoning them with discouragement and antagonism. I believe if most people knew what dire effects their bad dispositions have, they would try to correct them.

A bad disposition can be corrected. It is a habit, not an innate trait of character. Correcting it takes two mighty big qualities—intelligence and self-discipline.

We must thoroughly convince our-selves how well worth doing it is. We must face the fact that it not only harms others, even people who are dear to us and whom we do not want to harm, but that it harms ourselves. It lessens our appeal and our power. It makes us so disagreeable that others try to avoid us, losing priceless oppor-tunities for us. It lessens the love and companionship others could give us and thereby robs us of ordinary, run-of-the-mill happiness. It lessens our abilities, for no one can operate effi-ciently when his emotions are aroused by rage.

The clinching argument is its utter futility. It never corrects the condi-tions which arouse it. Does yelling at

Mary for breaking your best vase restore it? Does criticizing Johnnie for spending all his evenings away from home make him more anxious to stay in? Does nagging a husband for not making more money make him more capable?

All right then if you are convinced it is worth making the strenuous effort it will take to change your disposition, what can you do about it?

We could put the answer in two columns, the "stops" and the "starts." Stop doing the things you have been doing (the bad disposition things) and start doing the things you haven't.

Stop flying off the handle about every little annoyance. It's easy if you stop and smile when you first begin to feel cross.

Stop resenting. The more you do it, the more you have to resent. At first those affronts were unintentional —it was only your sensitiveness which made you even see an affront in them. But people get tired of handling you with kid gloves. After a while they'll stop trying to spare your feelings and will give you reason for resentment.

Stop sulking or being sullen. Half the time others don't know what you're sore about, so how can they correct it?

Stop criticizing and condemning. They don't correct. They only create resentment or fear which prevents correction. Thinking critically and condemningly stirs up your own ire and that's hard to stop after it gets going.

Stop being too severe. It doesn't prevent the other fellow from doing anything he greatly desires to do. It only stems the flow of confidences between you. Whether husband or wife or child, he or she will try to hide such acts from you and you'll wind up not knowing what's going on, deprived of such influence as you might have, and shut out from the warmth of family intercourse.

These are some of the "stops." You'll find them easier to observe if you bring your intelligence and sense of justice to the fore and realize that everyone is different. Everyone has his own pattern of thinking and living. His standards may not please you —but perhaps yours don't suit him, either. That doesn't alter the fact that each person has the right to be himself.

Again, I say that these "stops" will be much easier if you pause when you first find yourself starting to be annoyed. It isn't always possible to do this by sheer will power, but there's a priceless trick which *will* enable you to do it.

> • *A bad disposition can be corrected because it is a habit and not an innate trait of character. To correct it, you need to exercise your intelligence and some pretty stiff self-discipline. But it's worth it; it will pay dividends!*

Make yourself think of some good qualities in the annoying person. Or of something he has done for you, some good time you've had together. You can't mix oil and water. When you begin thinking of his good qualities you stop feeling annoyed at his bad ones and the moment passes without discord. Your actual *feeling* changes and you don't have to force it with will power.

Now for the "starts."

Start being patient. The other person will be so amazed and relieved at your understanding that he'll overflow with gratitude to you. You, yourself, will feel like a conquering hero for not having lost your temper.

Start being friendly—interested in the other person's opinions, problems, affairs. It will beget confidence in you and respect for you. It will knit a closer, sounder, richer relationship between you.

Start being courteous—as courteous to your family as to important business associates. It will alter the tone of your voice, change the look on your face, relax the tension of everyone present.

Start being appreciative. Appreciation is like sunshine—it makes things grow. Think how you swell and expand when you get it. So does the other fellow. Give him appreciation for what he has done and you will find him eagerly doing more to deserve more appreciation.

Sure these attitudes will require some pretty stiff self-discipline. But *they pay dividends!* They bring peace with yourself. A warm, glowing feeling of good will. An open, friendly relationship with those close to you, which draws them to you like a magnet. A happy, harmonious home, blessed with the sunshine of pleasantness instead of the misery of cold, repelling ill will, disapproval and discord. Children free to speak and act normally, to confide in you and to listen willingly to your best advice. A loving, companionable mate.

These results are worth working for. They are worth giving up some of your own desires, giving in on some issues, going out of your way to be pleasant. Just as a bad disposition does untold harm, a good one brings untold benefits.

YOU ARE YOUNG . . .

If you enjoy moving.

If the idea of losing your job doesn't strike you as fatal.

If you are interested in new inventions

If you can give up a proposed trip with the idea that there's no hurry.

If you never say to a younger person, "When I was your age."

If the experience you have gained is absolutely useless to you.

—*Magazine Digest.*

Published in Great Britain in 2014 by Old House books & maps
c/o Osprey Publishing, PO Box 883, Oxford OX2 9PH, UK.
c/o Osprey Publishing, PO Box 3985, New York, NY 10185-3985, USA.
Website: www.oldhousebooks.co.uk

A CIP catalogue record for this book is available from the British Library.

ISBN-13: 978 1 90840 276 9
Originally published c. 1944 by Arthur Murray.
Printed in China through Worldprint Ltd.

14 15 16 17 18   10 9 8 7 6 5 4 3 2 1